FAITH UNDER FIRE

STORIES OF HOPE AND COURAGE FROM WORLD WAR II

STEVE RABEY

OLIVER
NELSON
™

THOMAS NELSON PUBLISHERS®
Nashville

A Division of Thomas Nelson, Inc.
www.ThomasNelson.com

Published in Nashville, Tennessee, by Thomas Nelson, Inc.

Library of Congress Cataloging-in-Publication Data

Rabey, Steve.
    Faith under fire : stories of hope and courage from World War II / Steve Rabey.
        p. cm.
    ISBN 0-7852-6559-7
    1. World War, 1939–1945—Veterans—Religious Life—United States. 2. world War, 1939–1945—Religious aspects—Christianity. 3. World War, 1939–1945—Biography. 4. Christian biography—United States. I. Title.

D769.1 .R33 2002
940.54'78—dc21   2002007196

Printed in the United States of America

3 4 5 6 BVG 06 05 04 03 02

IN LOVING MEMORY
OF
WILLIAM E. RABEY

✶ CONTENTS ✶

INTRODUCTION

For many years, the people who lived through World War II were known as "the silent generation." And who wouldn't want to remain silent about some of the horrible things these men and women had experienced?

Then the 1990s brought a flood of words and images in the form of popular movies, books, and TV specials. These various projects resurrected long-forgotten tales of bravery and heroism and paraded them before new audiences, who surprised nearly everyone by their intense interest in these stories.

After international terrorists attacked America on September 11, 2001, many people seemed even more interested in knowing what life was like in the 1940s, a time when the entire world seemed poised on the brink of annihilation.

By now, some folks have had enough of the recent resurgence of reminiscing. Others argue that the so-called greatest generation's acts of courage and compassion will never be sufficiently celebrated. One thing is clear: many of the latest movies and books have largely ignored the important role that religious faith played in the lives of millions of men and women.

In 1942 an army chaplain named William Thomas Cummings uttered these memorable words: "There are no atheists in the foxholes." Although he may have been overstating matters, there's no overstating the powerful impact of faith for many of the men who fought in the war and many of the women who supported them and the war effort.

The goal of *Faith Under Fire* is to tell these untold stories of conviction and devotion. For a year, I sought out people who believe God miraculously sustained their lives during those trying times and who remain convinced that their faith in God has made all the difference in their lives ever since.

These stories feature evangelicals who endured injury or imprisonment only to return to foreign lands as missionaries. They feature Catholics, including a chaplain who ministered as bullets flew on Iwo Jima and a priest who risked everything to save hundreds of Jews from extermination. They feature mainline Protestants whose faith was refined in the fires of combat. They feature a veteran of the Tuskegee Airmen who says God's grace helped members of his all-black unit to withstand both German attackers and American racists. And they feature a Korean-born Episcopal priest who as a teen lied about his age to join the U.S. Army, a second-generation Lebanese immigrant who has been a major benefactor of his hometown Orthodox church, and the only Medal of Honor winner to have been a war deserter.

People welcomed me into their homes and their lives. Some gladly opened their scrapbooks, photo albums, or written memoirs; others held back tears as they unlocked memories that continue to haunt their dreams.

The first veteran with whom I met was a delight. He had prepared for our interview as if it were a college exam, and he promised to quickly read my draft chapter, letting me know about any errors or omissions I had made. Only two weeks later, he called from the hospital. In a voice that was barely audible, he apologized for not getting back to me as quickly as he had hoped. "I had a stroke," he said, laboring over every word. "I'm sorry I haven't called, but I promise I will call you as soon as I can."

I'm thankful that I was able to record this man's memories before they vanished from the face of the earth, which is what is happening to memories of more than a thousand World War II veterans on a daily basis. I'm also thankful for the opportunity to provide readers with these glimpses into the souls of these unique men and women.

The people whose stories are told in these pages were young when war broke out. They hadn't asked to have their lives interrupted by a world crisis, yet when crisis came, they responded. And clearly their faith in God was a significant—if little understood—part of their response.

I have grown from talking to these men and women. I hope you have a similar experience as you read their stories.

—Steve Rabey

ONE

MONSIGNOR PAUL BRADLEY

MINISTERING
AS THE BULLETS FLEW

The events of World War II were captured in thousands of photographs and hundreds of newsreels. But one image of the war stands out above all the others. It is a dramatic photograph showing six U.S. soldiers raising the American flag atop a rocky volcanic hilltop.

That hilltop was known as Mount Suribachi. For many people, Mount Suribachi isn't as familiar a name as Mount Everest or Mount Rushmore. But for historians of the war, the raising of the flag on this otherwise insignificant hill signifies the U.S. victory on Iwo Jima, which was one of the bloodiest battles in the entire conflict.

Iwo Jima, which is Japanese for "sulfur island," was a small speck of land that had immense strategic importance. Equipped with three airfields and located less than two hours' flying time from Japan, the island was a key part of the American battle plan.

The island was important to the Japanese, too, which is why they had invested in reinforcing its defenses. Though only eight square miles in size, Iwo Jima was fortified with nearly eight hundred concrete pillboxes, hundreds more caves dug into the volcanic landscape, large minefields and trench systems, and a network of underground tunnels that snaked through three miles of solid rock.

But it was more than physical fortifications that made Iwo Jima a hell on earth for American soldiers. More than twenty-two thousand dedicated Japanese fighting men defended the island.

The U.S. attack began with weeks of bombardment from the air. The next and most deadly phase began on February 19, 1945, with wave after wave of marine amphibious landings. Within a few days, the six American soldiers ascended Mount Suribachi and raised the Stars and Stripes for all on the island to see.

But this symbolic event didn't mean that the fighting was over. Instead, back on the beach, the carnage continued. It would be mid-March before organized resistance ceased. Most Japanese fought to the death, and only about two hundred surrendered.

Still, the raising of the flag was important, for it indicated not only that the battle on Iwo Jima was changing course, but also that the entire war in the Pacific was entering a new and decisive stage. Perhaps that's part of why the photograph of the six brave fighting men has become such a powerful part of the American psyche.

"Their collective image, blurred and indistinct yet unforgettable, became the most recognized, the most reproduced, in the history of photography," writes James Bradley in his bestselling book *Flags of Our Fathers*. Bradley's father, John, was one of the six men standing on top of Mount Suribachi that day. And as Bradley's book points out, the impromptu patriotic celebration atop the hill signaled the end of one of the most horrific battles in the history of modern warfare. In fact, Bradley calls the struggle on Iwo Jima "one of the great military slaughters of all history . . . It ground on over thirty-six days. It claimed 25,851 U.S. casualties, including nearly 7,000 dead."

But Iwo Jima represented more than mere carnage. According to Bradley, it epitomized American heroism. "More medals for valor were awarded for action on Iwo Jima than in any battle in the history of the United States," he writes. Or as Admiral Chester W. Nimitz, commander in chief of the U.S. Pacific Fleet, put it, "Uncommon valor was a common virtue."

One of the brave young men who received some of the awards handed out for bravery on Iwo Jima was Catholic Chaplain Paul F. Bradley (who is no relation to author James Bradley). Chaplain Bradley received a Bronze Star with a V for valor, as well as a Purple Heart for wounds he received on the island.

Armed with little more than holy water, some Communion hosts, and an immense faith in God, Chaplain Bradley made his way around the blood-soaked beaches of Iwo Jima, caring for and ministering to the many fallen men. The priest didn't wear a helmet. Rather, he wore a baseball-style cap with a gold cross stitched on the bill. "That way they could see me coming," he said.

Many of the men did see the priest making his rounds on the beach. And sometimes, between bursts of gunfire and mortar explosions, one could hear the men calling out to him: "Over here, Father."

Then, with bullets still flying, Bradley accompanied the men who ascended Mount Suribachi and, from a temporary table set up in a foxhole, offered Mass for the fighting men.

His sacrificial care for the men inspired the living, comforted the dying, and grabbed headlines around the world. But anybody who knows Bradley today knows that his life of courage and selfless service didn't end on that beach. Rather, it was just beginning.

FRONT-PAGE NEWS

"Chaplain Fights Way to Top of Mountain on Iwo to Say Mass," screamed the headline in the March 9, 1945, issue of the *St. Louis Globe-Democrat*.

"A few minutes after the American flag went up over the shell-torn crest of Mount Suribachi—even though Japanese still lurked in caves on the battered hillside—Navy Lt. Paul Bradley of Brooklyn, New York, a chaplain, said mass on the summit," wrote Sergeant Larry Schulenberg, a reporter for the *Globe-Democrat* who was on military leave on Iwo Jima and witnessed Bradley's bravery firsthand. He continued,

The ceremony was offered in honor of those Marines of the twenty-eighth regiment who had died capturing the fortress peak.

Father Bradley was with assault troops as they commenced the final attack on the bitterly defended mountain. He went up with the Marines, administering last rites to those who fell on the way.

The padre landed on D-Day with early assault waves and after serving at the front lines for several hours came down to the mortar-blasted beach to attend casualties brought in for evacuation to waiting hospital ships.

He performed his duties for two days and two nights without rest, and in the words of a naval medical officer, "Father Bradley did more for the morale of the wounded than half of the stuff we could give them."

At this writing Father Bradley is back on the slopes of the crest, moving slowly upward with Marines who are flushing Japanese out of deep, complex caves. Suribachi is still claiming casualties.

The *Globe-Democrat* and other newspapers around the country heralded Bradley's bravery. Or was it insanity?

Months later, the story had made it across the Atlantic to the *Ulster Examiner* from Bradley's ancestral home in County Omagh, Northern Ireland. "Said Mass Under Hail of Bullets," proclaimed the headline, while the story provided additional details about Bradley's compassionate care for wounded soldiers:

On the beach in the areas where wounded men were arriving by dozens was complete chaos. No tents, no cover—even plasma dressings and brandy were low. The first two boats bringing in badly needed litters were blown out of the water.

In that aid station, where some wounded men were being hit a second time as they lay helplessly awaiting evacuation, a naval doctor told of the job Father Bradley had done.

"In some cases," the doctor said, "we couldn't even give the wounded morphine. I asked Father Bradley to talk to many men who could not get the medical attention they deserved. He went from man to man, regardless of faith, spoke to them and tried to console them.

"He was kneeling next to one man with shrapnel wounds when a bullet from a sniper entered the man's side. Father Bradley didn't move.

"It was hours before we got the supplies we needed. We depended on him in that critical period."

The Irish paper's article concluded with final words of praise for Bradley:

The regiment's job is done. With them was Father Bradley, a young Irishman with the prayers of a Brooklyn mother behind him. He has seen many young men entering the Valley of Death.

It is true that he was their chaplain, but that was almost secondary. He was their friend.

What would make a man risk his life in such ways? Thinking back on those days, Bradley admits that the line between faith and foolishness is a thin one.

"If I knew then what I know now, I might have been more careful," he says. "But when you're young, you feel you're indestructible. I remember feeling, 'Nothing can happen to me.'

"Also, my faith was strong. And I have always inherently felt that when your time comes, you've got to be ready, for you know not when you will die.

"I've seen the strongest, healthiest guys get picked off with a direct hit, so it's not something you can control."

LIFE IN "THE MEAT GRINDER"

As the assault on Iwo Jima dragged on for weeks of grisly, hand-to-hand combat, the marines created a morbid nickname for the Pacific island where they fought: "the meat grinder."

Bradley saw more than his share of human misery, some of it beginning almost before he had even left his landing craft. "Our group had come to Iwo Jima on a merchant ship," recalls Bradley. "Then we all went down rope ladders to smaller boats that would be our landing craft. As the landing craft went right up to the beach, you could see the guys who had already been picked off."

Once on the beach, the horrors of war grew more intense. Bradley describes the scene: "You could hear the thud of the bullets hitting guys in the guts. I would kneel next to them and anoint them, regardless of their religion. I was taking care of anybody who was dying.

"At times I was practically lying on the island's black sand. I could maneuver myself around by kind of worming my way across the sand. I would lie low, sort of moving forward a bit, until I came across guys who had already been hit.

"I had a backpack that carried a Mass kit, and I would offer Holy Communion for those who were conscious. I also had anointing oil for those who were not conscious. It seemed that most of the men I saw at first had already lost consciousness."

As the fighting moved beyond the beach and across the rest of the island, the carnage continued. One soldier sat calmly on the ground smoking a cigarette, a blanket wrapped around him. When the blanket was lifted up, one could see that his legs and one arm were in tatters. The marine had stepped on a land mine.

Another time Bradley came across a squad of three or four marines with flamethrowers who had been using them to clear out some underbrush. But there had been a horrible accident.

"There they were," says Bradley, "and they were really burned. As I anointed them, one right after another, it was hard to find a place on their faces that was solid, really. They were gasping for life. One died while I was there, but before he passed away, he said, 'Thank you, Father.'

"That was a big difference from my later civilian life as a priest. Often, people seem to take the sacraments for granted. But on that day, here was a man who was dying, and he was thanking me."

Throughout such situations, Bradley was too busy to be diverted from his priestly duties. "You're so distracted in warfare, and so overcome with a resolute determinism and the intention of trying to do the best you can, that all you can do is stretch yourself around," he explains.

But on at least two occasions, Bradley stretched himself almost too far.

"I was moving across a hillside when all of a sudden, I sensed someone coming out of what turned out to be a cave and heading toward me," he says.

"On account of the fact that Japan didn't recognize the Geneva Conference's rules regarding warfare, chaplains in the Pacific were allowed to carry side arms. I pulled my gun and aimed for his midsection, but hit his leg.

"A very short time later, a U.S. intelligence officer said there had been Japanese hand grenades nearby. I look back at that now all these years later and wonder how differently things might have turned out."

And on one other occasion, Bradley became separated from his own men.

"I was near the front line a short time after Mount Suribachi had been secured. I assumed that the front line would be a straight line between the A Company and the B Company platoons, but I was wrong, and I was in no-man's-land. I was being peppered by Japanese rifles.

"I just played dead and didn't move for quite a while. When things quieted down, I made a beeline for what I thought was my own outfit again, and it was.

"I always felt that God was with me and protected me during these times. But I remember looking back after that last episode and saying, 'Gee, while I was playing dead I never even thought to say a prayer to God.'

"But I was just too distracted to pray. I was too busy trying to figure out which way I was going to run."

PRAYER AND DEATH

For some people, it may seem odd to think of a priest being in the line of fire. After all, aren't priests supposed to be pacifists? And aren't they supposed to be quiet and reflective rather than the companion of marines?

Anyone who knows anything about Bradley, his upbringing, and his calling to the priesthood will know that he's not the shy, retiring type. His father was born near Belfast, Northern Ireland, and as a youngster, he moved to New York, which is where he met Bradley's mother. As one of three children in a devout Catholic household, Bradley learned respect for God and country.

"I came from a home where daily prayer was an important part of my life," he recalls. "Morning and night prayers in the family setting promoted a great spirit of reverence toward authority, and especially the supreme authority, almighty God.

"And a natural consequence of my upbringing was that I also developed a deep love of family and a love of country."

Bradley's father rode a horse for thirty-two years as a mounted policeman.

"He did that in all kinds of weather. And I would say that of all the men I have met—and I have met some great men—my father was one of the sturdiest characters of them all. He was a real straight shooter."

His parents didn't pressure Bradley to become a priest. In fact, his mother seemed to want him to pursue a more "normal" line of work. And that's what he was intending to do when the call to the priesthood came.

"I was working part-time and going to college," he says. "I had a job at Rockaway Beach. I worked for the parks department, which supplied workers to monitor the playground by the beach for five dollars a day.

"One morning as I got to work, I looked down at the beach and saw that a body had washed up on the sand. Later I learned that it was a male who was in his twenties.

"This experience made me think about the important things in life. After that, I thought I would try being a priest."

He was ordained into the priesthood on June 7, 1941, which was six months before Pearl Harbor.

"War had broken out within the first year after my ordination, and there was a big need for Catholic chaplains.

"I had always had a deep love for God and country, and a great patriotic awareness. I knew that there would be a need for priests. And I knew that casualties would be heavy because of the instruments of war used in World War II.

"So volunteering to be a chaplain seemed to be the natural thing to do. I was just happy to get into the war and do my part as an American, as all Americans were doing," Bradley notes.

A LIFE OF SERVICE

Bradley wasn't hit by shrapnel until a day or two before the island was secured. But the injury didn't interfere with his career as a chaplain.

He served at sea, at air bases, and at a marine academy during the

Korean conflict and the Vietnam War. In 1967, Pope Paul VI bestowed on Bradley the rank of Domestic Prelate with the title of Right Reverend Monsignor.

He retired from the U.S. Navy in 1969 and was appointed pastor of St. Michael's Catholic Church in Long Branch, New Jersey, where he served for the next twenty years.

The transition to parish ministry wasn't an entirely easy one. For one thing, he missed the close friendships he developed in the military.

"People say marines are rough, but while they may be tough on the surface, I always found them to be good-hearted guys.

"And as an old confirmed bachelor and celibate priest, there are times when I can miss the camaraderie of being in the service. There was never a lonesome moment when I was serving in an outfit like the marines."

In 1989, when Bradley reached the ripe old age of seventy-five, he was required to retire. But you can bet he didn't give up the ministry. Instead, he transferred across town to St. John the Baptist Catholic Church, a primarily Spanish and Portuguese congregation, where he serves as assistant parish priest.

His two weekly English Masses fill the sanctuary, and some of the pews are filled by parishioners from St. Michael's who journey across town to be with their beloved priest.

In June 2001 the congregation of St. John's celebrated the sixtieth anniversary of Bradley's ordination. The guest speaker for the event was *Flags of Our Fathers* author James Bradley, and President George W. Bush sent a letter commemorating the occasion. "A strong spiritual foundation is central to the lives of Americans," read the letter. "Our nation is a better place because of your dedication to sharing your wisdom, guidance, and faith with others."

Even today, a nearly blind Bradley hasn't entirely laid down his backpack.

"I'm getting ready for another invasion," he says, "in the hereafter."

"Over here, Father!" Chaplain Paul Bradley's distinctive cap made it easy for the injured and dying men on Iwo Jima to spot him and call out to him for consolation.

Hilltop Holy Communion. Shortly after U.S. soldiers secured Mount Suribachi on Iwo Jima and raised the American flag for all to see, Father Bradley held Mass on the hilltop.

Returning to the scene. On February 19, 1965, Father Bradley (second from left) and other marines returned to Mount Suribachi to commemorate the twentieth anniversary of the beginning of one of the most horrific battles in the history of modern warfare.

A passionate priest. Returning to civilian life and ministry in New Jersey, Bradley remains a beloved priest.

TWO

BOB BOARDMAN

TELLING OTHERS ABOUT JESUS

When Bob Boardman talks, people listen very closely. They have to because this burly ex-marine speaks with a perpetually raspy whisper. (He says his voice sounds like a broken cement mixer.)

When those who don't know him ask if he has a cold, his response is quick: "No, it's my Japanese laryngitis, and it's not contagious."

On Father's Day, 1945, Boardman was driving a tank as part of the First Marine Division's attack on southern Okinawa. After a series of Japanese armor-piercing shells struck and disabled the tank, Boardman and three other surviving crewmen were attempting to make their way to safety when a bullet ripped through his neck. He knew something was wrong the moment he cried for help and no sound came out of his mouth.

His wounds were almost fatal. But that bullet didn't end his life any more than his neck injury stopped him from talking. He has spent more than three decades as a foreign missionary, and today he takes advantage of any opportunity he has to share the good news of Jesus Christ.

On September 12, 2001, he was at a Las Vegas hotel speaking at a reunion of the Marine Corps Tankers Association, a group for which he serves as chaplain.

The day before, terrorists had hijacked four American commercial airplanes, slamming one into the Pentagon and using two to destroy the Twin Towers of the World Trade Center. As he spoke one day after these shocking attacks, people listened to Boardman's words even more closely than usual.

"I had an unprecedented open door to share as I've never felt free to share before with this group," says Boardman, who now lives in Seattle.

"Listening in the audience were not only some two hundred marines and their spouses, but hotel employees. At that particular moment, just about anybody you met had become ultrapatriotic and quite open to hear about spiritual things.

"So I shared about how we are living on the edge of the last days. Soon, and no one knows precisely when, Jesus Christ is going to return to the earth to reign and rule in power and bring the ultimate peace that no one today seems to know how to attain or reach.

"I also encouraged everyone to look into the mirror of God's Word to see both themselves and our Savior, and to understand what's happening to us as a people as we live on the brink of the last days."

Boardman's novel voice can be heard as he occasionally performs funerals and weddings for veterans and their family members and as he regularly speaks to men's groups and at college campuses. Obviously he would never have asked for his injuries, but he accepts them with a certain sense of spiritual inevitability.

"My voice is unique," he explains. "It's something that I would not have chosen or thought of for myself, but God has fashioned things in this way, as if He put His finger through my neck for His purposes."

No More "Dog-Tag" Christianity

Like millions of Americans, Boardman was galvanized into action by the attack on Pearl Harbor.

"When Pearl Harbor took place, I was only seventeen and was working in the woods of Oregon as a lumberjack," he says. "Still, I wanted to enlist and get in on the excitement, the adventure, and the revenge. But if you were under eighteen, both parents had to give their permission. My mother refused to sign a consent form, so I had to wait until I was eighteen."

In the meantime, he enrolled at Oregon State College (now Oregon State University), where he played center and linebacker positions for the Beavers freshman football team. His schedule also included a girl-friend and a busy college social life.

As for church, it failed to hold much interest.

"I had been raised in a very formal type of Protestant church, and it really didn't have a clear explanation of the gospel. As I reached my early teens, I went to church less and less. I was involved in so many things that church just seemed irrelevant."

After he turned eighteen and finished out the school year, Boardman rushed to enlist in the Marine Corps, as had many of his college friends and teammates. But before he left Oregon for boot camp in San Diego, his parents asked him to visit church once more.

"My folks wanted me to be an official church member and to be baptized. So I agreed to do that. But nothing happened spiritually in my heart. It was mainly something I did for them."

His military identification dog tag had a space for recording his religious affiliation. The space was filled with a letter *P* for Protestant, but that didn't mean Christianity really had much place in his life. "For me at that time, all that *P* meant was that I wasn't a Catholic," he says.

After boot camp and infantry and tank training, Boardman shipped out to Australia where he and other new recruits would replace marines who had been wounded, killed, or struck down with malaria during the fierce fighting on Guadalcanal.

"We arrived in June 1943, but unlike San Diego, it was the middle of winter in Australia. Apparently the Marine Corps hadn't gotten the word on that, so we were all dressed in our summer khakis. We just about froze."

But there was no complaining because the new recruits wanted to impress the war-weary veterans, whom they regarded as heroes.

"We were in great awe of these combat marines, some of whom treated us like rookies are treated in the NFL," says Boardman. "We had to prove ourselves, and of course, the ultimate proof wouldn't come until after we had gone into battle, which is what we wanted. That was why we enlisted."

As Boardman argues in his book, *Unforgettable Men in Unforgettable Times,* there's a difference between real-life heroes, who have earned the respect they are given, and celebrities, who are often famous for little more than being famous.

"It's very clear to me that twenty-first-century America is a celebrity culture, which is a false culture," he says. "Many kids are growing up on that, and they don't know the difference between real heroes and celebrities.

"But events like the attacks on the World Trade Center make the differences more clear. In the aftermath of those attacks, there were so many modern-day heroes. There were also heroes on that hijacked flight that crashed in Pennsylvania. I hope with tragic events like these, the difference between heroes and celebrities has become clearer to our generation."

As Boardman and other green marines were trained and integrated into the First Marine Division in Australia, and as their initial introduction to real combat came ever nearer, so did concerns about matters of life and death that Boardman's superficial faith had done little to prepare him for.

Stationed in the little Australian town of Ballarat, he also found himself involved in a fistfight with an Australian soldier. Winding up his powerful right arm to deliver a decisive punch, he aimed at his opponent's head. But the Australian ducked, and Boardman's fist flew through a plate glass window, severing tendons in his wrist.

Lying in a hospital before he even had a chance to fire a shot at the enemy, Boardman felt miserable and humiliated. Teasing from his comrades added to his disgrace.

At the same time, there was a deeper anxiety gnawing at his soul. Boardman began to fear that he would die in combat. The fear threw him back upon the resources of his faith. But those resources were few indeed. The only prayers he knew were the Lord's Prayer and the children's prayer that begins with the words, "Now I lay me down to sleep."

Knowing that such a child-sized prayer was no match for his man-sized fears, Boardman began reading a Gideon's New Testament that a friend had given to him.

"I was really hungry to know God. Day by day God met my seeking heart and began to show me that Jesus Christ was the answer. That Jesus Christ, whose name I took in vain constantly, was the only One who could really help me."

Shortly before Boardman was shipped off to his first engagement with the enemy, he asked Jesus to come into his heart and guide his life. His newfound faith would be a powerful source of strength in the challenging days and years that lay ahead.

BOMBS AND COCONUTS

Boardman's first proving ground would be at Cape Gloucester on New Britain, the principal island of the Bismarck Archipelago northeast of New Guinea. There, where he was a member of the First Tank Battalion, the dreamy idealism he once had about war met the harsh realities of daily life as a marine.

"The terrain, which included rain forest, swamps, impassable dirt roads, and constant rain, limited the use of our tanks and other motorized vehicles," he remembers.

"The living conditions here were the toughest I faced in two years in the Pacific. Memories flood back of water-filled foxholes and jungle hammocks, which were a severe test of patience to string and then learn to get into! They often filled with water too. In time we learned that the rainwater would gradually warm up to body temperature and we could sleep on, though fitfully."

After they secured Cape Gloucester, the marines' next combat took place at Peleliu, a two-by-six-mile island located near the equator that was the site of one of the First Marine Division's bloodiest battles in the Pacific. It would also be the place where Boardman received his first combat wound and the first of two Purple Hearts.

"Our main objective was to capture the Japanese airstrip and neutralize that," says Boardman. "We did that the first day, but we battled to take the rest of the island for the next month."

Once the airfield was secured, it became a staging area for the tank battalion, which would move out across the island and return to the airfield for fuel and ammunition.

"One day as we were refueling and reammoing, I left my tank for a moment and walked out among the bombed-out remains of some of the Japanese airplanes. As I walked, I heard something directly over my head. It was an artillery shell that went whizzing past me.

"I hit the deck simultaneously with the explosion. I was lying prone, and either a piece of shrapnel or a chunk of the island's coral tore my arm.

"When I staggered out of the debris and headed back toward the tank, I was bleeding and covered with coral dust, so I looked like a ghost. My buddies thought for sure I was a goner. But a corpsman bound up my wound, and I went back into combat."

In time, resistance forces on Peleliu fell to the marines. In between engagements the fighting men were taken to Pavuvu in the Russell Islands for regrouping, retraining, and receiving replacements. Even on the seemingly safe staging island, the marines faced an unusual danger falling from the skies above.

"The island was home to a large Australian coconut grove, and some twenty thousand men pitched our tents between the symmetrical rows of coconut trees, which covered nearly six thousand acres.

"But we soon became highly aware of the dangers of falling coconuts. Several cases of concussion were awarded with something we jokingly called the Pavuvu Purple Heart."

THE FATHER'S DAY MASSACRE

Boardman's next assignment was Okinawa, where he would be hit with weapons much more dangerous than falling coconuts.

It was June 17, 1945, and the marines had been fighting it out on the island for seventy-eight days. The First Tank Battalion, which started with fifteen tanks, was down to three or four operating vehicles.

Boardman and the other four members of his crew were pushing into enemy-held territory just below Kunishi Ridge, a coral ridge reinforced with Japanese fortifications.

Soon, antitank armor-piercing shells began slamming into the tank. Boardman tried to turn the vehicle so that it faced the source of the fire, but one of the shells had knocked off one of the tank's metal tracks. The engine was running, but the tank was immobilized.

Boardman yelled up to the gunner, telling him where the Japanese were dug in. Just as he did so, one of the 76-millimeter shells pierced the turret, immediately killing the gunner, Robert Bennett from Oklahoma.

The shell also wounded tank commander Jerry Atkinson, who radioed back to company headquarters to request help even as shells continued to hit the tank. When Atkinson gave the order to abandon the tank, Boardman, his assistant driver, and a third crewman exited through their hatches. Atkinson pulled himself out of the tank and tumbled onto the ground, unable to move.

Boardman and one of the other men put an arm around Atkinson and began stumbling toward safety. As they made their way, they saw flames pouring out of the turret. They had escaped just in time.

But more dangers lay straight ahead. A Japanese sniper hidden in one of the island's hundreds of coral caves opened fire.

One fateful bullet went through the first soldier's chin, continued through Atkinson's neck, and passed through Boardman's neck, shattering his index finger after it emerged.

"It knocked us all down," says Boardman. "I still hadn't realized that I had been hit, but then I saw blood all over my jacket and on my hand. Then I noticed that I couldn't move just right.

"I tried to yell out, 'Help me,' but nothing came out. I remember opening my mouth to yell, and the other men's faces were filled with fear. They thought the commander and I were done for, so they made their way to safety.

"Next I realized that I was having trouble breathing. Soon, taking each breath was like what I imagined drowning to be. I was a new Christian, so in the simplicity of my faith, I thought it would be better to be with the Lord. I lay back, closed my eyes, and tried to pass out. But I couldn't.

"I decided to get out of there, so I began to crawl, holding my throat with one hand. I tried to make it up a ridge, but I didn't have the strength. I headed instead for a road, and soon I saw another one of our tanks coming my way. I waved my other arm at the tank, and thankfully they recognized me. I was weak from losing blood, but I managed to crawl onto the tank. Lying beside me was a dead crew member, Scuddley Hoffman from West Virginia, who was wrapped in an orange parachute."

Boardman was shipped out the same day to a hospital ship where his life hung in the balance for days. Doctors performed an emergency tracheotomy operation, and they also amputated his injured index finger. For more than a year and a half, he was shuttled between field hospitals and surgery centers before returning to Salem, Oregon, in February 1947.

He was awarded the Silver Star for his bravery in the face of enemy fire and his concern for his fellow marines, whom he helped rescue at grave personal risk.

A Reluctant Return to Japan

For nearly a year, Boardman received surgery in the Philadelphia Naval Hospital. While there, he went into town to attend local churches and participate in Youth for Christ rallies.

"I had a struggle with being willing to do what God wanted me to do," he says, "and during that year in Philadelphia, God spoke to my heart about foreign missions."

Boardman met a Christian girl named Jean. The two shared much together, but not his passion for mission work.

"I thought that whatever I did in life, she would be my wife and do it with me," he recalls. "But I discovered over a period of several months that that would not be. God wanted my unconditional surrender. I was trying to surrender to God with the proviso that if Jean would go with me to the mission field, I would go myself. Finally, by God's grace, I was able to lay that relationship on the altar. I told God that I was willing to go and do what He wanted me to do."

There were still two surprises in store for Boardman.

For one thing, he would meet another Christian woman named Jean.

"I didn't know God wanted me to change Jeans," he says, "but He had a designer pair in mind."

For another thing, he was being asked to serve as a missionary in Japan with the Navigators, a Christian group founded by Dawson Trotman and a group of military veterans and servicemen trained by Trotman.

"I really didn't want to see the Japanese once again after the war," Boardman explains. "Like most servicemen, I had been brainwashed to despise the Japanese. When the Navigators invited me to go to Japan, I could not say yes. I had a tremendous struggle with the Lord and fought Him in intense spiritual combat for about six weeks."

Ultimately Boardman surrendered this aspect of his life too. And to his amazement, he was able to forgive, and his love for the Japanese people rapidly grew.

"It came rather quickly and naturally, or even supernaturally," he says. "I had these misconceptions about Japanese people, and I had no idea what I would do or say when we met."

But Boardman found the words to say. After eighteen months of serving in Japan on his own, he married Jean Keith in Tokyo, and the two spent the first four years of their married life on the island of Okinawa. After that, they lived more than thirty years ministering to the former "enemy" in Japan.

STILL TALKING ABOUT JESUS

At a marine reunion held about thirteen years after the end of World War II, Boardman tried to tell some of his ex-comrades about his change of heart toward the Japanese and his decision to enter missionary service.

For his main illustration, he spoke about his fellow marine Bud Brenkert, who had once risked his life by covering Boardman's body during a Japanese sniper attack.

"Bud, you were willing to sacrifice yourself for me because we were good buddies from boot camp days. But would you do that for me if I was your enemy?"

Boardman then explained Jesus' sacrifice for all of humanity, including His enemies, as explained in Paul's letter to the Romans: "Very rarely will anyone die for a righteous man, though for a good man someone might possibly dare to die. But God demonstrates his own love for us in this: While we were still sinners, Christ died for us [Rom. 5:7–8]."

Boardman delivered this minisermon in his unique, raspy whisper. And as usual, people listened closely to take in his words.

THE WARRIOR'S PSALM

When Bob Boardman was fighting on the Pacific island of Peleliu, dread was a constant companion.

It was a fearful place, he says. The island was a big coral rock, and the Japanese were hidden away in five hundred coral caves, both natural and man-made. We had to rout out the enemy cave by cave.

When he had a spare moment, Boardman consoled himself by reading the small Bible he had been given. As he made his way through the Psalms, he found solace in one particular psalm that spoke to his fears.

It was Psalm 18, and an introductory note to the psalm indicates the conditions under which it was written: [David] sang to the LORD the words of this song when the LORD delivered him from the hand of all his enemies and from the hand of Saul.

Psalm 18 was my constant refuge on Peleliu, says

Boardman, who was challenged to place his ultimate faith in God, his Rock, and not be intimidated by the rock caves that threatened him daily.

He still refers to the passage as the Warrior s Psalm, and he turns to it often, both when he is speaking to the public and when he seeks reassurance of God s presence in his life:

I love you, O LORD, my strength.
The LORD is my rock, my fortress and my deliverer;
    my God is my rock, in whom I take refuge.
    He is my shield and the horn of my salvation, my stronghold.
I call to the LORD, who is worthy of praise,
    and I am saved from my enemies.
The cords of death entangled me;
    the torrents of destruction overwhelmed me.
The cords of the grave coiled around me;
    the snares of death confronted me.
In my distress I called to the LORD;
    I cried to my God for help.
From his temple he heard my voice;
    my cry came before him, into his ears.
The earth trembled and quaked,
    and the foundations of the mountains shook;
    they trembled because he was angry.
Smoke rose from his nostrils;
    consuming fire came from his mouth,
    burning coals blazed out of it.
He parted the heavens and came down;
    dark clouds were under his feet.

He mounted the cherubim and flew;
  he soared on the wings of the wind.
He made darkness his covering,
    his canopy around him
    the dark rain clouds of the sky.
Out of the brightness of his presence clouds advanced,
  with hailstones and bolts of lightning.
The LORD thundered from heaven;
  the voice of the Most High resounded.
He shot his arrows and scattered [the enemies],
  great bolts of lightning and routed them.
The valleys of the sea were exposed
    and the foundations of the earth laid bare
    at your rebuke, O LORD,
    at the blast of breath from your nostrils.
He reached down from on high and took hold of me;
  he drew me out of deep waters.
He rescued me from my powerful enemy,
  from my foes, who were too strong for me.
They confronted me in the day of my disaster,
  but the LORD was my support.
He brought me out into a spacious place;
  he rescued me because he delighted in me.
The LORD has dealt with me according to my righteousness;
  according to the cleanness of my hands he has rewarded me.
For I have kept the ways of the LORD;
  I have not done evil by turning from my God.
All his laws are before me;
  I have not turned away from his decrees . . .

You have delivered me from the attacks of the people;
  you have made me the head of nations;
  people I did not know are subject to me.
As soon as they hear me, they obey me;
  foreigners cringe before me.
They all lose heart;
  they come trembling from their strongholds.
The LORD lives! Praise be to my Rock!
  Exalted be God my Savior!
He is the God who avenges me,
  who subdues nations under me,
  who saves me from my enemies.
You exalted me above my foes;
  from violent men you rescued me.
Therefore I will praise you among the nations, O LORD;
  I will sing praises to your name.
He gives his king great victories;
  he shows unfailing kindness to his anointed,
  to David and his descendants forever.

Copies of Bob Boardman's book, *Unforgettable Men in Unforgettable Times,* are available from the author for $17 (softcover) or $24 (hardcover). You can also request copies of Boardman's tract, "I Was a Dogtag Christian." Write to P.O. Box 25001, Seattle WA 98125-1901.

In the Marines—Galvanized by the Japanese attack on Pearl Harbor, Bob Boardman left his college football team to enlist in the Marines. Assigned to the First Marine Division, Boardman endured intense fighting and suffered a life-changing injury.

Heroes or celebrities? Boardman believes many of the men he fought with in World War II deserve the title "hero," a title that became more popular after the terrorist attacks of Sept. 11, 2001.

"Hopefully, with tragic events like these, the difference between heroes and celebrities is becoming clearer to this generation."

★ THREE ★

NEWT HEISLEY

AN ORDINARY HERO

The flag has a black background that draws the viewer's eye to the stark illustration at its center. There, a profile of a young man's head is flanked by barbed wire and a guard tower.

It's the POW/MIA flag, and according to the *Washington Post*, it flies at hundreds of locations throughout the country, representing the pain and anguish of those who have loved the eighty-eight thousand U.S. men and women missing in U.S. military actions, most of them from World War II.

The humble man who designed the flag is as self-deprecating about it as he is about his own service in World War II.

"I'm no war hero," says a sincere Newt Heisley. "I'm just an ordinary guy who did my job and was lucky to come home."

Technically speaking, he might be right. Unlike some of the other people featured in this book, Heisley didn't storm fortified bunkers or risk being pierced with bayonets. But like many of the others whose stories are told in the following pages, he did leave loved ones, a job, and the comforts of home because his country needed him. In answering the call to serve, he performed many acts that can best be described as heroic.

The action he faced wasn't the pitched battles on enemy lines. Rather, First Lieutenant Newton Heisley of the U.S. Army Air Corps piloted huge transport planes that carried paratroopers to their missions, provided support to the frontline fighters, and removed the injured to safety.

On the other hand, he did have his share of close calls that forced him to grit his teeth and move on by sheer force of will as he ferried cargo from air bases in New Guinea and the Philippines to landing strips throughout the Pacific.

KAMIKAZES AND HURRICANES

During the months of April, May, and June 1945, American forces targeted the Pacific island of Okinawa. Located some 350 miles off the Chinese coast, Okinawa made a good spot for launching attacks on the Japanese mainland. The island was also a key communications link in Japan's far-flung fighting forces.

Heisley flew many loads of supplies to Okinawa. After delivering one load, he prepared to bed down in his sleeping bag, creating an impromptu spot underneath one of the wings of his massive plane, which was parked next to a military airstrip.

He was about to climb into his sleeping bag when he heard the drone of an airplane engine still far off in the distance. Within seconds, his quiet little outpost was a bustle of activity as searchlights scanned the sky for the incoming Japanese attack plane.

Looking up, Heisley saw a kamikaze pilot aiming straight toward him. There was no time to do anything but jump for cover, and as he did so, he heard an explosion. The suicide bomber had missed Heisley's plane but scored a direct hit on the wing of the plane parked only a few feet away.

"It's fortunate that he didn't hit the gas tank, or I might not have made it out of there," he recalls.

Another close encounter was even more bizarre. That time, the danger came not from human enemies, but from the forces of nature.

Heisley had made a cargo drop on Ie Shima, the tiny island located a few miles off Okinawa where famed war correspondent Ernie Pyle had been killed. There U.S. pilots slept in tents and huts, not under the wings of their planes.

But those very accommodations could be turned into death traps when the typhoons that spun out of control above the Pacific touched down on specks of land like Ie Shima.

Typhoons are tropical cyclones that cover as much as five hundred miles and have winds circling at up to seventy-five miles per hour. The typhoon that struck Ie Shima the night Heisley was there flattened tents, collapsed the mess hall, and transformed sheet-metal roofing into lethal scythes that cut down everything in their paths, including trees and men.

LONG, LONELY FLIGHTS

Surviving typhoons and living through a kamikaze attack aren't the kinds of things that generate newspaper headlines. Nor are the long cargo runs Heisley flew, some of which took him and his crew hundreds of miles out over the lonely Pacific. But the flights regularly exposed him to danger and possible death. The fear he and his crewmates experienced during those long, lonely flights caused them to think about what would happen if the plane lost power and disappeared into the ocean.

If they were really lucky, rescue teams would find the men. And luck would be needed. "The Pacific is a *big* ocean," observes Heisley, "and rescue teams, if any were available, would be hours and hours away.

"In addition, during our flights, we routinely checked in with a U.S.

submarine stationed somewhere south of Okinawa. But even if we failed to check in on time, it's not certain the sub's crew would summon a rescue team to look for us."

Heisley certainly faced his share of wartime challenges, but he isn't the kind of person to trumpet his accomplishments. He resists numerous requests to talk about the Bronze Star he received. (Despite repeated questions, he declines to reveal what kinds of bravery the medal honored.)

"When I finally came home, my wife hung out my service jacket on the laundry line to air it out," he says. "My neighbors were impressed by all the ribbons on the chest of that jacket."

But Heisley's innate modesty prevents him from being overawed by his accomplishments in the heat of battle and repeatedly insists that he isn't a hero. Still, his service to his country and much of his life ever since have exhibited numerous qualities of the heroic, which one dictionary defines as "having or displaying the character of a hero: extraordinarily bold, altruistic, determined."

COMMITTED TO BROTHERHOOD AND COUNTRY

Newt Heisley was born in 1920 in Williamsport, Pennsylvania, where he inherited both Christian principles and American values. His parents and grandparents were Lutherans, and his grandfather was particularly devoted to his faith.

"I can remember as a child the many trips we took to market four miles away," says Heisley. "As we rode behind Dewey, the family horse, my dear grandpa would quietly whistle or sing the only songs he knew—the hymns of the faith."

Farther back on the family tree, another relative played an important but largely unacknowledged role in the Protestant Reformation. Johann Fust loaned money to Johannes Gutenberg, the fifteenth-century

German printer whose revolutionary printing press used movable type to print Bibles in the German language.

As a child, Heisley didn't rebel against the faith of his family, although he did exhibit the typical youngster's interest in more active pursuits.

"I preferred softball to Sunday school," he says. "Sometimes some of us kids would head over to the sandlot in our Sunday clothes. When we saw the cars leaving church, we would stop our game and dash back to the church."

Heisley is committed to the fundamentals of the faith, and he has been a loyal member of First Presbyterian Church in Colorado Springs since 1972. He holds his principles loosely rather than using them to assault others.

"I believe implicitly in Jesus Christ," he says, "but I might be considered a little radical in some ways. Brotherhood is my faith. I never make the statement that something is 'the Christian thing to do' because I have found that that's offensive to people who are non-Christians."

The main way Heisley expresses himself is through his beautiful paintings. Sitting in his living room, one can see his deep appreciation for people whose traditions and cultures are different from his own.

One painting shows a scene from *Madame Butterfly,* an opera by Giacomo Puccini about a young Japanese girl who was deserted by her lover, an American naval officer.

"It's one of my wife Bunny's favorite operas," he notes. Even more than that, the painting shows Heisley's tender affection for the Asian people, some of whom were his fiercest enemies during the war.

Another painting is a bold, dignified portrait of a Pawnee Indian chief.

"We sponsored his son, who was a student at the nearby Air Force Academy," explains Heisley.

His motto in regard to other human beings is one of acceptance and love: "Basically I don't care if someone is green or Greek."

These attitudes were part of the values Heisley inherited from his family and the many other German immigrants who populated rural Pennsylvania.

"My father's parents were farmers who held the basic American values of hard work and honesty. Even though they were poor and were barely able to keep their farm, they believed in honest dealing with everyone."

His mother died when Heisley was only sixteen weeks old, so he spent much of his childhood with his mother's parents. Although they lived in the city, they honored the same values.

One relative in particular inspired Heisley's youthful dreams.

"Uncle Ray was a real role model. He was an athlete, a great patriot, and a brave warrior who had fought in World War I. He was fifty-five when World War II started. He wanted to reenlist with the U.S. Army, but he was too old. He said they didn't want him, and he threatened to join the French foreign legion instead. Finally they appointed him to a position overseeing the acquisition of steel for the war effort."

After high school, Heisley went off to Syracuse University, graduating with a fine arts degree. His first job out of college was selling boys' clothing for a department store.

His next job enabled him to use his fine arts training. He was hired on as a graphic artist in the advertising department of the *Pittsburgh Post Gazette.*

"It was a good job, and I was making thirty-five dollars a week," he says.

But after the Japanese attacked Pearl Harbor, Heisley knew he had to enlist.

"Actually I was ashamed to not be involved, but it was mainly patriotism," he says. "I felt I needed to be doing that job. I'm not sure I would have felt the same about Vietnam, but World War II was different. I had to serve.

"It was also a great opportunity to fly. Up until that time, I had never been up in a plane. But that would change soon."

SURVIVING IN THE AIR

Heisley had always wanted to pilot planes, and once he volunteered to fight in World War II, he had plenty of chances for that.

Following basic training, he reported to Ellington Field in Texas for flight training school. There he received his Air Corps wings and the gold bars of the second lieutenant. He was qualified to fly seven different types of military aircraft.

Flying was easy, but landing the big military craft was a different matter altogether. "If you can survive your own landings, you breathe a sigh of relief," he says.

Heisley shipped out to Asia in March 1945, and almost immediately he was piloting the Curtiss C-46 Commando, a giant, whalelike aircraft that, at the time, was the world's largest twin-engine transport plane.

His first assignment was to New Guinea, one of the largest islands in the world. From 1942 to 1945, the mountainous island was a fierce battleground between Japanese forces and soldiers from Australia and America. By 1945, Japanese forces were largely contained, and Heisley was flying missions in his big C-46.

Next stop was Leyte, an island in the Philippines. American troops fought there from October to December 1944. And the nearby Leyte Gulf was the scene of a decisive naval battle that effectively ended the Japanese Imperial Navy's era of sea superiority.

"We were hauling in supplies, ammunition, bombs, and food," he says, "and taking out the wounded and paratroopers."

By 1945, Okinawa had become an increasingly important island for U.S. forces. The attacks on Japanese positions there began on April 1. Progress was slow because of the island's rough terrain, and the Japanese had created a formidable network of defenses including caves dug into the hard ground.

The fighting was intense and continued through June 21, with Japanese dead estimated at more than 100,000. Many Japanese had committed suicide rather than turn themselves over to the victorious U.S. troops.

Heisley wasn't involved in the combat, but provided the support that made victory possible. "Fortunately I never had to kill people," he states.

Still, the carnage he saw on Okinawa haunts him to this day.

"I saw bodies strewn everywhere," he recalls. "There were dead Japanese, and in some cases just skulls. You don't have to see much of this kind of thing to be shocked."

As a result, Heisley refuses to revisit these painful memories by watching war movies.

"I won't look at those things," he emphasizes. "I've had enough war. I'm not interested in that. I want to laugh and smile and take care of Bunny, who is my inspiration in life."

Although thankful for the Allied victories, Heisley frequently thought about the horrendous wastes of war.

"That was the awful thing," he says, "the total waste of it all. I remember flying over Hiroshima several times after the atomic bomb had been dropped. I didn't fly very low, but I could still see the destruction, which was horrendous."

Heisley doesn't consider himself a pacifist, but he does have a deep respect for life in all its forms. When an insect invades his house, he transfers it back to the great outdoors instead of killing it. The thought of humans killing other humans bothers him even more.

"The Japanese people were very likable," he says. "Their children were a joy. To kill people of any society bothers me deeply."

Even after a kamikaze pilot had tried unsuccessfully to crash his plane into Heisley's aircraft and sleeping bag on the island of Okinawa, he thought about the waste of it all.

"I didn't take any joy in the fact that he had killed himself. Instead, the first thing I thought was that this was some Japanese mother and father's son," he remarks.

"War is a shame. Whether it's Palestinians and Jews killing each other, or the troubles in Ireland, year after year, people keep murdering each other."

Of course, Heisley certainly didn't want anyone murdering him, so throughout his service, he prayed to God.

"I prayed every night and usually more than once a day," he recalls. "My prayer was: 'Get me home to my wife, please, God, and preferably in one piece.'

"He must have been listening to those prayers. It's almost eerie sometimes when you get results from a prayer."

GROWING FROM HIS EXPERIENCES

War may be a horrible waste, but World War II had its benefits for Heisley.

"The cadet training was the most fantastic thing I ever went through," he reveals. "I also learned tremendous discipline. I remember one night when some of us were given privileges to go to a nearby town for some rest and recreation. This was highly unusual to be allowed out at night. Unfortunately I was ten minutes late coming back to base. The next day, I marched for ten hours to make up for my mistake. I was seldom late for something during the rest of my life."

Heisley also believes that by being forced to confront some of his deepest fears—including the fear of sudden death—he emerged from the war stronger and more confident.

"It reinforced my thoughts that I could do things I didn't know I could do," he says. "I'm just an ordinary guy, but even to get through cadet training was an accomplishment. An awful lot of people got washed out, yet I made it through gritting my teeth and forging ahead.

"My father always told me there was no such word as *can't*. Today I tell my little nine-year-old granddaughter that she can be anything she wants to be."

FLYING THE FLAG FOR POWs AND MIAs

After piloting cargo planes and serving as part of the army of occupation in Japan, Heisley returned home to his wife and college sweetheart, Bunny. He also returned to his work as a graphic artist, this time for Hayden Advertising, an agency in New Jersey.

One of the agency's clients was the Annin Flag Company, which at the time was the world's largest maker of all kinds of flags. In 1971 a group from Jacksonville, Florida, called the National League of Families of American Prisoners and Missing in Southeast Asia, contacted the agency.

They represented some of the thousands of American servicemen who had been lost in action or imprisoned in Vietnam, and they wanted a flag they could use to promote their message. Heisley gladly accepted the assignment to design the flag.

As he thought about the project, he reflected back to his days flying huge transport planes across the Pacific. Flights of four hundred miles or more were routine. Some of the longest flights were nine hundred miles or more. Much of the time, the plane traveled over the Pacific Ocean, whose massive size both impressed and concerned Heisley and his crewmates: copilot Robert Frey, navigator William Wennberg, radio operator Frank Holloway, and crew chief Willy Swor.

"We flew all over the South Pacific, from the northern Philippines to Okinawa," he reports. "Most of the time we were looking for islands that didn't even rate a dot on a world map.

"We hadn't received much training about what to do if the plane went down in the water, so there was a fair amount of anxiety. Someone

FEARLESS OR FOOLISH?

Newt Heisley insists that he s not a hero. Still, he routinely volunteered for missions that would put him in harm s way. One particular mission might have ended his life had he been permitted to tackle it. He tells the story:

One day there was an announcement. Some of our guys were stuck on some godforsaken Pacific island. The commanders wanted someone to fly in and rescue them using a naval-type amphibian craft.

I had never flown one of these craft. In fact, I had never even seen one up close. Still, I wanted to help out, so I foolishly volunteered to take the mission. I ll fly it, I said.

Someone else in our group volunteered to fly the rescue mission. He had actually flown the type of amphibian craft that was being used, so the officers gave the assignment to him. I don t know what happened because I was out of there the next day.

Later on, I did have a chance to fly one of the amphibian craft. It was a piece of cake. But I didn t know that when I volunteered.

once said flying is hour after hour of boredom interrupted by moments of sheer terror. We certainly had our share of terror during those flights. We all knew there were parachutes somewhere in the back of the plane, but mainly it was a lot of good old American optimism that kept us going.

"I remember a particular flight. On that day, we were flying to Okinawa.

Formosa was off to our left somewhere about four or five hundred miles. I remember thinking that it would have been easy for the Japanese to shoot us down. I felt like we were a sitting duck in this big cargo plane.

"I began to wonder what would happen to me if I was taken prisoner. I wondered how I would conduct myself. And I thought about how the worst thing that could possibly happen would involve being taken prisoner and being left and forgotten somewhere.

"As I began to work on rough sketches for the flag, that experience came back to me, and I wrote down the phrase, 'You are not forgotten.'"

The phrase stuck. Then all Heisley needed was a visual image. He thought he would use a figure in silhouette, and in the background would be a guard tower. For the silhouette, Heisley used his son Jeffrey, then twenty-four, who had just returned from marine training sick and underweight.

"If he didn't look exactly like a prisoner of war, he was the next thing to it," Heisley remembers.

The client loved the design, and in time, POW/MIA groups from other American wars embraced the flag. Now the flag flies for nearly ninety thousand missing.

Over the years, Heisley's POW/MIA flag has become nearly as ubiquitous as the Stars and Stripes. For the past three decades, it has flown throughout the country he fought to defend. In 1988 it flew over the White House. The next year, it became the only flag ever permanently displayed in the Capitol Rotunda.

In the 1990s Congress passed a law requiring that the flag be flown on six annual holidays at numerous government facilities. The holidays are Armed Forces Day, Memorial Day, Flag Day, Independence Day, Veterans Day, and national POW/MIA Day, which is September 17. The facilities where it is flown include national cemeteries, military bases, veteran memorials, and all U.S. post offices.

Although Heisley never served as a prisoner, his work on the flag has made him sort of a hero to supporters of the POW/MIA movement. Of course, he would deny once again that he did anything unusual. But for this veteran, ordinary acts seem heroic enough.

A flying whale. Heisley piloted a Curtiss C–46 Commando, a huge cargo plane like this one, during the war.

An ordinary guy a long way from home. Heisley, shown in his pilot's uniform, smiles before taking off for a training mission.

"You Are Not Forgotten." Newt Heisley's long flights across the Pacific in a transport plane provided the inspiration for the POW/MIA flag, which he designed in 1971. Today the flag is the nation's most popular flag after the Stars and Stripes.

FOUR

CHARLES DRYDEN

FIGHTING TWO WARS

When veterans of World War II meet to share their experiences, among the first questions they ask each other are: In which branch of the service did you serve? And in what theater did you serve?

For Lieutenant Colonel Charles Dryden, Retired, such questions are simple to answer. He was a pilot in the Ninety-ninth Pursuit Squadron of the Army Air Corps. And he flew missions in North Africa and Sicily.

But other issues are much more difficult for Dryden. Like hundreds of other African-Americans, he was a member of the Tuskegee Airmen. Although they fought against the enemy with bravery and valor, the black airmen always felt as though they were fighting another war too.

"We were fighting two wars," says Dryden, "one abroad and one at home. And the one at home was against Jim Crow."

Many people look back to the early decades of the twentieth century as some kind of golden age in America. And looking back, we can see that life does seem to have been simpler then for many people, and that religious values played a greater role in daily life than they do today.

For African-Americans, though, the first half of the century was no paradise. The segregationist Jim Crow laws noted by Dryden kept Southern blacks locked into a system that was separate and unequal. It's ironic that America, a country that went to war to defend freedom and democracy around the world, would deny full freedom and equality to some of its own citizens.

That was the way things were when Charles Dryden and other pioneering black men joined the U.S. Army. But their devotion to duty and their dedication to the democratic values that America itself didn't always observe helped change the country for the better.

History or Hollywood?

In the summer of 1995, cable network HBO aired *The Tuskegee Airmen*, a film starring Laurence Fishburne, Cuba Gooding Jr., and Malcolm-Jamal Warner. Produced with a small budget by the network itself, the film didn't win any major awards. But it did tell a fascinating story that had not been told in the movies before.

As Detroit journalist Curt Schleier put it, "*Tuskegee* tells the story of a remarkable group of men who became the first African-American fighter pilots in the U.S. Army Air Corps. Ironically, to fight for their country, they first had to fight their countrymen, some of whom didn't believe blacks were smart enough or brave enough to fly."

In the film, Gooding plays a fictional character named Billy "A-Train" Roberts. But Charles Dryden is the real "A-Train," as he demonstrated in his book, *A-Train: Memoirs of a Tuskegee Airman*, which was written in 1991 and finally published in 1997 (University of Alabama Press).

"I was born and raised in New York City," says Dryden, "and I was very familiar with the subways Duke Ellington sang about in his song, 'Take the A-Train.' Duke Ellington was my favorite orchestra all the time I was growing up. So when I finally got my own P-40 fighter plane, I named it *A-Train*."

In the HBO movie, the Tuskegee Airmen are aeronautical hotshots, one of whom flies low over the ground, buzzing the air base where he was training. The character dies in a gigantic fireball as his plane crashes into a building, but Dryden didn't die when he buzzed the Walterboro Army Air Base in South Carolina during the war. Instead, he was court-martialed, though he was not kicked out of the service.

"About 90 percent of the film is true," observes Dryden. "The rest is pure Hollywood."

Still, Dryden and other airmen applaud HBO's efforts to tell the previously little-known story of black Americans who participated in a historically important "experiment."

At a time when many Americans considered blacks inferior to whites and assumed they couldn't be trusted to perform well in the heat of battle, these brave black airmen fought tremendous odds to earn the privilege to risk their lives for their country.

Or as they sang in "The Fighting Ninety-Ninth," the official song of the Tuskegee Airmen:

> Contact—Joy stick back
> Sailing through the blue
> Gallant sons of the Ninety-ninth
> Brave and tried and true
> We are the Heroes of the night—
> To hell with the Axis might
> FIGHT! FIGHT! FIGHT! FIGHT!

By the time World War II was over, the Tuskegee experiment was a smashing success. Here's how journalist Curt Schleier summarized the airmen's achievements:

Despite numerous obstacles, 450 eventually made it to combat overseas, and between May 1943 and June 1945 were awarded more than 850 medals. None of the bombers they were charged with escorting were lost to enemy aircraft. And 66 of the Tuskegee Airmen made the ultimate sacrifice for a largely uncaring nation.

Generations are now largely unaware of the cruelty with which white America treated its black minority. Those unfamiliar with the contributions of these brave men need to see this film to learn about an important part of our past.

Dryden is quick to add that those who want to know more of the details about the airmen should read his book, which he describes as "a historical drama":

A drama with a story line about the "Tuskegee Experiment" in which the ability of "Negroes" to fly airplanes as pilots and to keep them flying as mechanics, armorers, radiomen, and the like was doubted, and tested.

A drama describing the continuing plot to dump the "experiment" in a dustbin of history.

A drama in which the villain of the piece was Jim Crow.

A drama in which the villain appeared often, and oftentimes unexpectedly, in the form of various "ugly Americans."

FAITH AND FLYING

Tough times test people's characters, and the challenges Charles Dryden faced in and out of the military demonstrated how well he had been raised by his parents, Charles Levy Tucker Dryden (nicknamed Brother Rob) and Violet Adina Buckley Dryden (Sister Vie).

Dryden's parents met and married in Jamaica, where both worked as teachers, before moving to Manhattan and having three children. Charles was born September 16, 1920, and living was far from easy.

"I was raised during the Depression, and there were times when Dad had to hold down three jobs in order to make ends meet. My parents always said that we never owned a car or a house, but they invested in their children. In time, all three us of went on to get master's degrees and achieve some success in different fields."

Dryden remembers his parents with deep affection: "Mom was the gentlest, most devout, loving mother anywhere, ever. Dad was Dad. Not Pop. Not a take-me-out-to-the-ball-game sort of father and yet not a rigid disciplinarian.

"Together Mom and Dad emphasized four things in my rearing: love and serve God, obey your parents, be loyal to your family, and get a good education."

Faith was not only an essential ingredient of his parents' lives; it was also an important part of how they raised their children.

"My parents were such devout Christians that they passed this on to my brother and sister and me. From my youngest days, we always attended Sunday school, and I had the guidance of my parents, my aunts, and other relatives, who were my role models."

It wasn't only family members who helped raise Charles, but members of the family's extended New York community.

"I was raised in an urban area of Manhattan and the Bronx, and I can truly say that in my case it took a village to raise a child. I grew up in a four-square block in which all the adults knew who I was, they knew who my parents were, they knew where I went to school and to church, and they really nurtured me."

In those days right and wrong were taught and practiced, not debated. "Children were disciplined," he says. "Girls held their particular virtues as a treasure. People waited for marriage instead of living together, as so many young people do today."

A Soldier in Search of the American Dream

In the epilogue of his book, *A-Train: Memoirs of a Tuskegee Airman,* Charles Dryden reflects on the words of British statesman Edmund Burke, who said, To make us love our country, our country ought to be lovely.

As Dryden says, America has both its lovely and its ugly sides, but that doesn t dim his faith in its highest ideals:

Those words, written by Edmund Burke about his country two centuries ago, are just as true today about mine America. America, the beautiful, about which a patriotic paean proclaims: Thine alabaster cities gleam / Undimmed by human tears . . .

Would that it were true that no tears were ever shed anywhere, anytime in its history, caused by affronts to the dignity of its citizens of color, or by assaults upon their person.

How lovely would my country be if its actions did not belie its brave words that all men are created equal and that in this land of the free there are liberty and justice for all! . . .

With the Germans and North Koreans I knew for sure who my enemy was. With many fellow Americans I was not at all sure!

However, I am certain about some things:

First of all, in spite of the many ugly Americans I have encountered who savaged my spirit by their bigotry, there have been a number of lovely Americans who salvaged my self-esteem by their decency. There come to mind Mary Elizabeth Sullivan, teacher in sixth grade; Agnes L. Mackin in junior high school; college professors Mario Carbone and Herbert Rosenbaum; civilian flight instructor Bill Pryhota and military flight instructors Clay Albright and Robert Rowland; senior military officers Noel F. Parrish, Arthur C. Clark, and James C. Truscott.

Second, I am certain America was changed somewhat by the achievements of the Tuskegee Airmen during World War II and thereafter as evidenced by the desegregation of the armed forces by President Truman. With that establishment of equal opportunity for all military personnel, three Tuskegee Airmen were promoted, subsequently, to the rank of general officer: General Daniel James, Lieutenant General Benjamin O. Davis, Jr., and Major General Lucius Theus. America seemed lovely then.

Third, I was certainly privileged to be a part of the Tuskegee Experiment.

Fourth, and finally, I most certainly am enormously proud to be a Tuskegee Airman!

(From *A-Train: Memoirs of a Tuskegee Airman* [Tuscaloosa: University of Alabama Press, 1997], epilogue)

The faith Dryden received from his parents not only gave him a strong moral code, but it also gave him a deep sense of inner strength that helped him cope with the difficulties of growing up poor and black in an increasingly affluent and predominantly white America.

"The faith bred into me was such a personal one that early on I had a strong belief that the Almighty, or the Divine, was very personal and very close.

"I knew that God had communicated His will to humans in the original Ten Commandments, and that Jesus had boiled them down into two:

"Love the Lord your God with all your heart and with all your soul and with all your mind." This is the first and greatest commandment. And the second is like it: "Love your neighbor as yourself." All the Law and the Prophets hang on these two commandments. (Matt. 22:37–40)

"That kind of upbringing impacted all my life and made it less difficult for me to live with and cope with the meanness and mean-spiritedness I encountered.

"Over the years, I've been hurt. And I'm human. At times I've been vengeful. But it has been a fairly easy journey for me through life with that kind of faith."

Dryden was a youngster when his love of aviation first started to blossom. His favorite hobby was building model airplanes. They weren't the plastic planes that came in kits and were ready to glue together. No, the planes began with blueprints pinned to a tabletop. And once he cut out and assembled the framework, he carefully covered the wings and fuselage with thin tissue paper that was made taut by sprinkling it with warm water.

In his spare time Dryden read magazines, books, and any other printed materials about planes he could get his hands on. A favorite pulp magazine was called *G-8 and His Battle Aces,* which featured the exploits of a fictional American World War I pilot.

After graduating from Peter Stuyvesant High School, Dryden attended City College of New York, which started a Civilian Pilot Training Program during his junior year. Dryden passed the program and received his pilot's license, but there was little he could do with it.

"Neither the U.S. Army Air Corps nor any airline was open to

African-American pilots," he recalls, but he visited an army recruitment office anyway. The man in charge said, "The United States Army is not training any colored pilots, so I can't give you an application."

Only months later, Dryden read in the *Bronx Home News* that Congress had just passed a bill authorizing the War Department to accept applications from "Negroes" for aviation cadet training.

Dryden read the article on a Saturday, so there was nothing he could do until Monday. But when Monday arrived, he showed up at the recruiter's office before it opened at 8:00 A.M.

Months later he received a letter from the army. Dated August 19, 1941, the letter told him to report for the Air Corps Flying School in Tuskegee, Alabama. Dryden's twenty-one-year military career had begun.

IN THE ARMY NOW

Dryden took a train out of New York for Washington, D.C., where he would transfer to a southbound train to Atlanta. Throughout his lengthy trip, he was forced to ride in "colored" cars and use "colored" rest rooms in stations along the way.

His government-issued ticket authorized him to eat meals in the train's dining cars, but even there, he was seated at a table that featured a green curtain. With the curtain pulled down, Dryden got to eat his meal, but was hidden from the other diners in the car, all of whom were white.

Racism didn't end once he arrived at the camp in Tuskegee. Some of his commanding officers were sympathetic, including Colonel Benjamin Davis, who would later become the Air Force's first black brigadier general.

Others, however, were less helpful. Some of the white officers even let it be known that they considered the Tuskegee "experiment" a major mistake and hoped it would be over as soon as possible.

The first class of thirteen black cadets reported to Tuskegee on July 19, 1941. Dryden and ten other cadets were part of the second class. Following eight months of training, only eight of the twenty-four initial cadets would graduate.

Some of the young men failed to meet the program's demanding physical requirements. Others never measured up to the army's strict qualifications for pilots. And others grew tired of the constant pressure to prove themselves.

Dryden persevered. When he received his pilot's wings, he felt a surge of pride. He couldn't wait to share his excitement with friends and family members back home.

"As I reviewed the life I had lived since my birth, I realized I had been able to achieve my life's ambitions by the time I was twenty-two," he says. "I was so excited that my heart was beating like a trip-hammer. I thought I was going to die with my heart beating out of my chest.

"I went home on leave, and as I listened to the clickety clack of the train wheels, I kept repeating to myself, 'I'm one of eight. I'm one of eight. I'm one of eight. I'm one of eight.' By the time I got back to Penn Station in New York, I almost couldn't stand my own conceit."

As soon as he stepped off the train, Dryden was quickly brought back to earth.

"A little old white lady came toward me and said, 'Here, boy, carry my bag.' I drew myself up to my whole five-foot-ten-inch height and said, 'I'm an officer in the U.S. Army Air Corps. What you want is a porter.'"

There are some people who would have lashed out in anger after such an encounter. Others would have retreated into their own private world. But Dryden, thanks to his upbringing and his faith, was able to see things in a bigger perspective.

"I had been getting too big for my britches, and she was an angel in disguise who brought me down to earth and made me realize that the uniform I was wearing didn't make me invincible.

"I had encountered racism early on in life, ever since I was in kindergarten. I can't say that it never disturbed me, but thanks to my upbringing, I learned to be introspective. I learned to examine people and situations for what they were, and to learn from that. It's something black people in America learn very quickly."

AFRICA, SICILY, AND BEYOND

During their time at Tuskegee, the men were visited by heavyweight champion Joe Louis, jazz singer Lena Horne, and other black luminaries. Dryden also had a chance to meet George Washington Carver, the pioneering agriculturalist who had experimented with sweet potatoes.

On another occasion, a visitor came all the way to Tuskegee to see Dryden. But the timing was bad—Dryden got word of the visitor right before a movie was to be shown on base.

"I was going to see a movie and grumbled all the way to the visitors' lounge. But when I walked in and saw my pastor from the Bronx, Rev. Elder Garnet Hawkins, I completely forgot all about that movie," says Dryden. "He told me he had been in the area on business and thought he would drop in and see one of his flock. We talked until lights-out that night. He showed me that he cared.

"Reverend Hawkins was one of the most devout and genuine clergymen I have ever met. Unfortunately not all ministers fulfill that role. Race doesn't matter. We all know various ones who have misbehaved. But Reverend Hawkins was truly a man of faith. He didn't just talk the Word, he lived the Word, and he was a mentor for me and about twenty of my peers."

Dryden and the other Tuskegee Airmen were getting anxious to see action overseas. Finally they were assigned to North Africa, where they would escort and protect Allied bombers.

"We provided escort for B-25 and B-26 medium-altitude bombers.

We were involved in dive-bombing enemy positions and strafing enemy troops with our machine guns. We also had our share of air battles with the Luftwaffe."

The airmen performed similar missions in Sicily, accompanying B–17's and B-24's, which were vulnerable to enemy attacks, on their long bombing runs.

By the time war was over, the Tuskegee Airmen had been so successful that none of the bombers they escorted were lost. Dryden declares, "A lot of the white servicemen didn't believe we could fly, so we said, 'We'll show them.'"

Their deeds are honored at the U.S. Air Force Academy in Colorado, where a statue of a Tuskegee Airman stands in the school's Honor Court. The inscription at the base of the statue summarizes their achievements:

> They Rose From Adversity
> Through Competence, Courage,
> Commitment, And Capacity
> To Serve America
> On Silver Wings, And To Set
> A Standard
> Few Will Transcend.

But when Dryden and seven other airmen were sent back to America as combat-tactics instructors during the war, old problems resurfaced.

At Selfridge Field in Michigan, the black airmen were denied entry to the base's all-white officers club. And at Walterboro Army Air Base in South Carolina, blacks were segregated in the movie theater on the base.

To make matters worse, black airmen couldn't eat in the "whites" food line at Walterboro, even though German prisoners of war could. Dryden wrote about the experience in his memoir: *We Were Insulted and Humiliated in Our Own Native Land!*

Finally, on July 26, 1948, President Harry Truman signed Executive Order Number 9981, which mandated the desegregation of the U.S. armed forces.

Looking back, Dryden knows that the Tuskegee "experiment" was an essential step in this process. And he is grateful for the role that he and the other airmen performed. Yet he can't deny the bitterness that lies buried deep within his heart: "As I think about some of the things we endured, tears of rage still begin to well up in my eyes."

LEAVING A LEGACY

Dryden went on to serve in Korea and at a number of domestic posts before he retired as a lieutenant colonel in 1962.

Since his book was published in 1997, Dryden has done hundreds of book signings around the country. Whether these events are held at bookstores or on military bases, they always attract veterans who want to meet and greet Dryden.

During a signing at Fort Bliss, Texas, Dryden was approached by a white veteran who had something to say.

"One day I was on a bombing mission over Vienna," said the man. "Our B-17 was being shot up pretty bad by enemy fighters. We were in trouble.

"Our pilot called for help, and in a few minutes, a couple of planes with the Tuskegee markings arrived and escorted us all the way safely home. If it hadn't been for you men, I wouldn't be here today. Our entire family owes you men our past, our present, and our future."

Thinking about that moment, Dryden says, "Accolades are like the air authors breathe, but you can't get any better accolades than that."

Still, when asked what his lasting legacy will be, Dryden turns from his military career to his family.

"The thing I have done that means the most is raising my three sons because they will be living into the future," says Dryden, who was slowed by a stroke in March 2001.

"I've tried to pass on to them the values that had been passed on to me by my parents. That's the reason we're born into this world, to hopefully contribute something to make it better than when we came into it.

"If, Lord willing, I have been able to pass on to my three sons those values I hold dear, that is the greatest role I've had to play in this life."

A statue of a Tuskegee Airman. The statue stands in the Honor Court at the U.S. Air Force Academy.

A love for flying. Neither the army nor the commercial airlines accepted black pilots, but Charles Dryden enrolled in a Civilian Pilot Training Program at City College of New York anyway. He is shown here in 1940 with a training plane.

A dream come true. Dryden graduated from cadet training on April 29, 1942, becoming the eighth Tuskegee Airman.

A distinguished career. By the time he retired from the United States Air Force in 1962 after serving his country for more than thirty years, Dryden was a lieutenant colonel. Still, he says his life's greatest accomplishment is his investment in his sons. "If, Lord willing, I have been able to pass on to my three sons those values I hold dear, that is the greatest role I've had to play in this life."

FIVE

FATHER BRUNO REYNDERS

A RIGHTEOUS GENTILE

Michel Reynders was only ten years old when German forces entered his native Belgium in 1940 as part of the Nazis' western offensive. The boy didn't know precisely why his land had been invaded. Nor did he understand the finer points of National Socialism. All he knew was that the enemy was now in charge, and that life was harder, food was scarcer, and people were more cautious about what they did and said.

There was one other thing Michel noticed. Beginning in 1942, his beloved uncle Henry seemed to be frequently running into people who needed help.

Michel remembers one of the many times when Uncle Henry approached him and sought his assistance.

"'Hey,' he asked me, 'do you have an hour this afternoon to help someone?'

"'Yes,' I told him, 'as soon as I am through with my homework.'

"'Good. I have a little guy who needs to go to the end of town. He doesn't know that part of town, but you do. Could you take him down there on the streetcar?'

"'Yes,' I said."

Uncle Henry wrote down an address and gave it Michel, who escorted the boy to a home and thought little more about it.

Michel also remembers the three women who stayed with the family in their house in the city of Brussels.

"They were just people who didn't know where to go and needed a room," says Michel, recalling what he had been told at the time. "They helped keep the house clean. They told us stories. Then gradually they disappeared."

It would be four long years before the Germans left Belgium. And it would be years later that Michel began to understand the truth about Uncle Henry. Now the nephew talks about his uncle whenever he can. And when he does so, it's with a sense of urgency.

That's because Uncle Henry, who was better known to people in Brussels as Father Bruno, risked his life during the war years to save more than three hundred Jews from almost certain extinction at the hands of the Nazis.

"My uncle has been a role model for me throughout my life," says Michel Reynders, who has lived in the U.S. since 1961, teaching at the University of Colorado School of Medicine and serving as an honorary vice-consul of Belgium.

"I have often asked myself a question: If I was in the same situation, would I have the courage to do what he did? I don't know. But I know I have a deep personal admiration for him because he was a person who did the right things."

OTHER SCHINDLERS

Many people have heard of Oskar Schindler, the German industrialist whose efforts to save hundreds of Jews were described in the novel *Schindler's List*, written by Irish author Thomas Keneally. In 1993 director

Steven Spielberg turned the book into a powerful and disturbing movie that introduced millions of people to the horrors of the Holocaust and won seven Academy Awards and numerous other honors.

Schindler may be the best known of the *righteous Gentiles,* the term Jews apply to non-Jews who risked all to save Jewish people. National Socialism, the political ideology developed by Adolf Hitler, emphasized racial purity and declared that no Jew could be a German. In the 1930s Germans had allowed some Jews to emigrate. But in 1941, the Nazi regime began implementing its Final Solution. By war's end, between four and six million European Jews had been annihilated.

These numbers would have been even higher had it not been for people like Oskar Schindler and Father Bruno Reynders. The two men pursued similar ends but with radically different means.

"I saw *Schindler's List* two or three times, and I admire Schindler very much," says Michel Reynders. "He took enormous risks to shelter the many Jews who worked in his factories.

"Whereas Schindler used power and money to get things done, my uncle didn't have a penny to himself. He had to beg right and left for everything he did."

A MAVERICK MONK

Henry Reynders was born in 1903. His parents were devout Catholics who brought up all eight of their children in the faith. Still, that background didn't prevent Henry from being a prankster. At school, he often served detention for acting up, and at home, he disobeyed his parents' orders to eat what he had been served and instead hid mussels under the dinner table and later buried them in the family garden.

As a child, Henry dreamed of being a soldier or an adventurer. At the same time he excelled at academics. The last thing anyone expected was the one thing he announced he would do. At age seventeen, he told his family he would become a monk.

In 1920 Henry became a novice. Two years later he made his solemn vows, and in 1928 he was ordained as a priest in the Benedictine order, taking the name Father Bruno. (No one is certain why he was given this name, but there was an eleventh-century monk who is now honored as St. Bruno.)

Like their founder St. Benedict, Benedictines typically spend more time in their monasteries than they do out in the secular world. But Father Bruno was different. For the next decade he traveled throughout Europe to study and teach. At one time, he even called himself "the most mobile Benedictine in Belgium."

Throughout that time, Father Bruno stayed close to his family in Brussels.

"He baptized me, and he married me," recalls Michel Reynders. "All that time in between, we saw each other as often as his ministerial duties allowed. I think he needed that occasional family contact to be able to withstand the austerity of the monastery."

Some people picture priests as cold and aloof, but Michel remembers his uncle as a different kind of monk: "He was a radiant person. He was gently pastoral, not at all someone who was pompously lecturing people on why they had to be good.

"There was something radiating out of him. He always had a half smile, and it wasn't an ironical smile. It was a compassionate, friendly smile. He also had a terrific sense of humor, and when he was with the family, we were always having fun and he was always telling stories. In between the wisecracks he would become more serious and talk about serious things."

In time, serious things would increasingly weigh on Father Bruno's heart. War was coming, and in its wake was the evil of anti-Semitism.

WAR ON THE JEWS

In 1938 the mobile monk was in Frankfurt, Germany. For the first time, the true horrors of the Nazi ideology became clear to him. Here's how he described this revelation in his memoirs, which he wrote in 1971:

My first contact with Nazi persecution dates back to July, 1938. Traveling through Frankfurt, I was strolling in a busy street. Everywhere I saw insulting signs, including one that read: "Jude = Judas."

It shocked me greatly, but what truly revolted me was the following incident. I saw an old man arriving, bearded, dressed in a caftan, wearing an old black hat, in short the stereotyped Jew.

This man walked stooped, not daring to raise his eyes, hiding his face with his hand. Passersby walked away from him as if he had the plague, or they bullied him, or pointed a finger and sneered at him.

This really upset me, this segregation, this contempt, this arrogance, this cruel stupidity. No, it was unbearable! It still lingers in my memory and makes me nauseous.

In 1939 war broke out in Europe, and Father Bruno became Chaplain Reynders, serving in the Belgian Fourth Artillery Regiment. Wounded in the leg and captured by the Germans, he spent a year in a prison camp, where his sense of humor and his kindness toward fellow prisoners won him many friends.

Returning to civilian life in 1942, Father Bruno was assigned to serve as the chaplain at a Catholic home for the blind. Once at the home, he made a surprising discovery: some of the residents at the home could see perfectly well. In fact, the home was a covert operation that hid Jews who were in danger of being arrested.

No one knows if Father Bruno would have saved Jews had he not been assigned to the home, but once he became chaplain there, he devoted himself to the cause.

By the end of the year, some of the Belgian adults affiliated with the house were arrested by the Gestapo. They included the heroic lawyer Albert Vanden Berg, who later died in one of the Third Reich's concentration camps.

Deciding that the home was no longer a safe enough hiding place, Father Bruno contacted private citizens to see if they would be willing to open their homes to the remaining Jewish children.

With those humble beginnings, Father Bruno began a new phase of his life. During the next two years, he would save between 320 and 350 Jews from certain capture and possible death.

RIGHTEOUS RESISTANCE

The Germans had occupied Belgium during World War I, so its citizens were skilled in the arts of resistance. Between 1942 and 1944, Father Bruno would travel hundreds of miles on his trusty bicycle, knocking on people's doors and begging them to take in Jewish children as well as adults. He never encountered a closed door, and although he was betrayed to the German authorities, he was never caught or punished.

"People helped my uncle for a variety of reasons," explains Michel Reynders. "Belgians value their independence. Also important was the fact that we were occupied, and by definition, those who were persecuting the Jews were our enemies too. Also, some helped the Jews out of a strong commitment to the values of the Christian faith."

Father Bruno's memoirs record many examples of people who, inspired by the sacrifice of Jesus on the cross, sacrificed their own safety to save others.

In one case Father Bruno visited Professor Luyckx of the University of Louvain. The priest made his case to the professor and waited in silence for a response.

"Professor, may I ask what your answer is?" he finally asked.

"But, Father, I am awaiting yours. You told me things of which I was not aware. I probably should have known them, but I was honestly ignorant. Why did you come and see me? Because you know that I am a Christian. You pointed out my duty as a Christian. So my answer is: When are you bringing me the Jewish child?"

Once, a newspaper reporter asked Father Bruno to explain why he—a Christian—helped save Jewish children. His answer was a concise summary of his practical theology:

> The motivation is rebellion against injustice and violence; awareness of our common past, both historically and theologically; and a personal liking for "meetings of the souls" at the "fringes."
>
> The goals are to save human lives; restore families; and establish human contacts between Judaism and Christianity.
>
> The spirit is one of respect for human life; respect for human dignity; mutual expansion and respect through a greater and mutual knowledge of our values, culture, and spiritual background.

RISKY WORK

Father Bruno risked his life to find families who would open their homes to the Jews. Beginning in January 1943, he had to find houses for ten children who were no longer safe at the home for the blind.

But Father Bruno had to find more than housing. He had to secure food for growing boys and girls at a time that all supplies were being rationed. Ration cards and stamps had to be illegally acquired with the help of municipal officials. Shoes and clothing were constant needs too.

MEMORIES OF AN "ALUMNUS"

Bernard and Charles Rotmil were two of the young Jews rescued by Father Bruno Reynders and the many Belgians who supported his clandestine operations. Here, in his own words, are Bernard Rotmil s recollections:

My Dad, a Jew residing in Belgium during the occupation, had finally been caught by the Gestapo at the end of June 1943. I was a young teenager short of 17, and my younger brother was 12. We already had lost our mother and our older sister. We were all alone. Father Bruno was a Benedictine monk who resided at the monastery located in the picturesque and very medieval City of Louvain. I told my brother that I would go and check it out and ordered him to wait for me on the stoop of our building. I would return by the evening at the latest.

After announcing myself at the monastery and explaining my desire to see Father Bruno, I was ushered into a small side room. Soon I became attracted by a small noise by the opposite door from whence I had entered. I noticed a peep hole and saw a blinking eye looking through. I got a bit nervous.

Suddenly, the door opened and there appeared before me a lanky priest with long and black flowing cassock, his hands were concealed inside it. Behind his spectacles shone vivid and intelligent eyes that seared through you and sized you up with a smirk.

He sat down across the table and asked for my

name and then let me speak. I immediately trusted him and felt his empathy. I explained to him my predicament and as he listened his eyes mellowed and I could sense great relief, that I had come to the right place. When I told him that I had left my brother at the stoop of our house he immediately got up and made note of the address. He didn t want to waste any more time and needed to go and pick him up right away. He told me he would be back shortly and took off in a huff. Father Bruno placed my brother with a family, while I was given a private room in the home of Mademoiselle de Bruyn, a lovely and distinguished lady. She already was housing three Dutch refugees who had the money to pay her for their upkeep. I did not have any money and had to pay my way by performing light house chores. From there I was sent to a Catholic parish house in Namur, a lovely town by the river Meuse.

We were provided with food stamps and false identity cards. Father Bruno was an active member with the underground and obtained for us false identification papers. My name became Bernard Roumieux, and I carried that name through the end of the war.

Over the coming months, I would stay in various private and religious houses, meeting fellow Jews who were being protected by Belgium s righteous gentiles.

During these days, Father Bruno was active day and night, cycling from one farm to another attempting to find a family who would take on some of his older children as farmhands. He remained in constant communication with me and I must say that his kind regards toward me meant so much during these times of alienation and danger.

I had an unlimited appetite and wore out my shoes of ersatz leather at a fast clip. He reminded me that his moneys were limited and to watch my appetite and be careful with my shoes. After the war there is a paragraph in his diary that refers to that admonition. He quotes my response: But Father I am so hungry! In response Father Bruno wrote these words in his diary: I was so touched by that response that I never brought that subject up again.

Father Bruno was always busy cycling to find homes for his children and occasionally he would stop by to pay me a visit at the farm he had found for me. He had a very laconic sense of humor and could be a lot of fun. I am proud to notice an entry in his diary that he found me to be a great companion. Because of him, I was fortunate to get my first introduction to Plato and metaphysics.

In fact, it was through the dedication and humble work of this Benedictine Monk that I shaped much of my philosophy of life. He was not only a brave man who had several narrow escapes, but he had an uncommon social conscience and always allied himself with the underdog first with the hated Jew and then with humble workers of Paris.

He was a man of God. He was intrinsically and essentially Christian, as he lived the life of Christ and truly relived His sufferings. It is in him that I saw that essentially pure aspect of the faith of that Jew from Galilee.

Overcome by his generosity, my brother and I felt as if we were becoming Christians, and I asked him to baptize us. To my great surprise he declined to do so without the consent of our parents. Most other clerics would have jumped at the chance of saving the soul of two children, but this man saw beyond the stricture of his faith and knew the underlying reason for our request.

I was saved by the good offices of Father Bruno and many Christian families of Belgium who risked their lives to save their fellow human beings.

While war and persecution had shown me the uglier aspects of humanity, it is the likes of Father Bruno who opened my eyes to the presence of good and heroic people and the ultimate triumph of good over evil.

In many cases the children made do with ill-fitting clothes and shoes fashioned out of cardboard.

The financial demands of the operation were a constant burden for a monk sworn to live a life of poverty. Even more important, the hidden Jews needed false identification papers with acceptable Aryan names.

The requests for help continued to stream in. In April 1943, homes for sixteen people were needed. The next month, seventeen more Jews required housing. November 1943 was the biggest month yet. Twenty-seven requests for housing must be taken care of immediately! While dozens of local citizens agreed to care for one Jew, many took responsibility for more than one. Father Bruno's own mother cared for as many as eight children at a time, and his brother Jean kept more than two dozen, some for lengthy periods of time. One valiant widow placed more than fifty children, escorting them to welcoming houses throughout the country.

The more deeply Father Bruno got involved in the work of righteous resistance, the more he stuck his neck out to make sure the operation kept working.

Living in a house that had been loaned to him and was located next door to a Gestapo commander in charge of the local Jewish affairs office, Father Bruno often hid children in his own home for several hours at a time until more permanent arrangements could be made. The celibate monk even "adopted" a wife and family to assist him in his efforts at escorting children.

In one elaborate episode, a Jewish woman whose children were sheltered by the priest offered him a large diamond to cover some of his expenses. There was only one problem: the jewel was in the lady's apartment, which had been sealed by the Gestapo.

The priest considered removing the paper strips that served as the Gestapo's seal, thinking he could replace them later. Then he considered climbing into the apartment through a window, but the caretaker wouldn't allow the priest to use his ladder. Father Bruno never got that diamond.

There were many close calls, but a combination of God's protection and the priest's radiant manner saved the day.

In one case Father Bruno was arrested during a Gestapo raid. He was found to be carrying a stack of blank identification cards, but he was able to talk his way out of the jam. He convinced the officers that he was a city worker who was simply taking home some of the cards so he could work on them during the evening hours. The officers let him go.

In another case the priest's politeness and patience saved the day.

Father Bruno regularly stopped at a Food Service Office, which controlled ration cards and stamps. One day as he waited in line, he saw a woman enter the office who seemed to be in a hurry. He let her take his place in line. When he reached the front of the line, the Food Service Office worker who cooperated with the priest couldn't contain his relief.

"This is a bit of luck," said the worker. "Do you see that fellow?" he asked Father Bruno, pointing to a man who was on his way out of the office.

"He's a Gestapo man checking on ration cards. One minute earlier and we were caught, you and I!"

"WHAT DID I DO?"

In September 1944, Brussels was finally liberated from the Germans. Among the Jewish survivors Father Bruno had helped was the Grand Rabbi of Liege, along with his elderly parents.

Some of the Catholic priests and nuns who helped rescue Jewish children believed it was appropriate to evangelize and convert the children to Christianity. But Father Bruno was adamant that his associates not do that.

After the war, Father Bruno worked to reunite the children with their missing parents. There were happy reunions, but many children never found their parents again. Many of the children stayed with the families who had cared for them during the war.

The end of the war did not mean the end of Father Bruno's military service. He again served as a chaplain to the Belgian troops, that time as part of the occupation force in northern Germany. The tour of duty exposed him to the horrors of the Nazi death camps and crematoriums. The priest who had been nauseated by the memory of Germans in Frankfurt taunting a Jewish man recoiled at the horrifying magnitude of the Final Solution.

By 1948 Father Bruno returned to his life as a priest, and until his death in 1981 at the age of seventy-eight, he served God and others with energy and compassion.

He seldom talked about himself, and he never sought the praise of others. Nevertheless, others praised him anyway.

In 1964 he received a supreme honor. The Israeli government inducted him into the Yad Vashem, or Avenue of the Righteous, a garden park that commemorates righteous Gentiles who helped the Jews during the Holocaust. He was a guest of honor of the Israeli government for two weeks, and during that time, some of the Jews who had been rescued through his work attended a reunion in his honor.

"What did I do?" he asked during a brief acceptance speech in which he characteristically tried to shine the spotlight on others, not on himself.

"I searched, but searching without finding is perfectly fruitless. Finding was not my doing. Finding meant that doors were opened, the door of a home, the door of a heart. Those who welcomed were nearly all those I approached and it is them I represent here."

Over the years many of the "alumni" of his rescue efforts wrote to him, telling him about their lives and thanking him for his sacrifice.

"I know all that you have done for us," wrote one widow. "Believe me, I shall never forget."

Father Bruno's funeral eulogy called him "a man of study and prayer, a man of action and perilous commitments, a man impassioned with God." The eulogy also summarized the priest's radiant attitude: "His kindness and humor reflected wonderfully the compassion of his Lord."

A decade before he died, friends and family members persuaded Father Bruno to begin writing down the amazing story of his life. Today, nephew Michel Reynders cherishes these memoirs. As he holds the volumes in his hands, he thinks about the lasting impact of that life.

"We are constantly reminded by members of the Jewish community that the Holocaust should not be forgotten. Thanks in part to Uncle Henry's work, perhaps it won't be."

"A radiant person." Father Bruno holds nephew Michel Reynders in 1935. Today, Michel tells others about his uncle's sacrificial work on behalf of Belgium's Jews.

"What did I do?" When Father Bruno was honored by the Israeli government in 1964 for his work during World War II, he characteristically tried to shine the spotlight on others, not himself.

Grateful beneficiaries. In 1994, seventeen of the Jewish children who had been rescued by Father Bruno gathered in Belgium to honor him. Nephew Michel Reynders is shown wearing sunglasses in the back row. Bernard Rotmil is at the far left. His story is told in this chapter.

A tree of life. Father Bruno plants "his" tree at Yad Vashem, the Avenue of the Righteous, in Israel. Standing nearby are supporters and some of his "alumni."

SIX

COLONEL LEWIS MILLETT

A SOLDIER'S SOLDIER

The vast majority of the millions of men who fought in World War II were civilians. These men left their peacetime lives when they enlisted or were drafted. And after the war, those who were still alive and able to return to normal lives gladly embraced civilian life once again.

Not Lewis Millett, a man who felt he had been destined to serve the country he loved by fighting in its armed forces during World War II, the Korean War, and the war in Vietnam.

A descendant of American fighting men going all the way back to the Revolutionary War, Millett has received many awards for his service, including the Distinguished Service Cross, the Silver Star, the Legion of Merit, the Air Medal, the Purple Heart (with three oak leaf clusters), and the Vietnamese Cross of Gallantry.

Millett also received the Medal of Honor, America's highest military honor, for his heroic deeds at Korea's Hill 180, a strategically important site that lay sandwiched between warring Chinese and North Korean forces.

At least they called it Hill 180 before Millett arrived there. As you will see, due to his bravery there, the site is today remembered as Bayonet Hill.

Now in his eighties, Millett is a regular feature at military reunions and commemorations, where his speeches routinely bring many members of his audiences to tears.

In 1998 Millett revisited Bayonet Hill for a ceremony honoring the men who died in the brutal battle that took place there. In his comments he expressed some of the deeply held values that have inspired him throughout his exceptional life:

> I have fought in three wars in seven different countries, visited with kings and commoners, soldiers and strangers. Of all the people I've met, civilians or soldiers, through all these wars, they have all only wanted one thing—to be free and to live in peace.
>
> But, the price of freedom comes very high. We've lost soldiers, sailors, airmen and Marines, not only fighting for their own country but for the freedom of other people.
>
> I hope all of these young people standing here today realize that the freedom they enjoy was paid for by the high price of blood, sweat and tears of people who died on the battlefields. The troops who died not only here, but also on the other battlefields did not die in vain. They died so you and I could live in freedom.

A Grandson of Soldiers

Lewis Millett was born on December 15, 1920, in Mechanic Falls, Maine. By the time he was seventeen, he had joined the National Guard with the 101st Field Artillery, Massachusetts. Those who knew him weren't surprised, for Millett had been groomed to follow in his ancestors' footsteps.

"In our family we've always been citizen soldiers," he says. "It's a tradition. And I believe that if you're a descendant of warriors, you are bound to be one."

He wasn't really pressured to be a military man. Instead, it was a desire he absorbed from being around members of his family.

"I can remember sitting around bonfires on the beaches of Maine. The water was cold, and the air was brisk, and we youngsters would listen to family members talk about how they had served in various wars.

"And on the Fourth of July, rather than go to a parade in town, we would get together as a family. There would be fifteen to twenty of us, including grandfathers and uncles.

"We kids would roast hot dogs and marshmallows, while adults would have lobster. And we would talk about how the thing that made America great was that we're a free country, and the reason we're a free country is because we fought for that freedom."

For Millett, patriotism isn't something he learned; it is something he inherited.

"I'm a Yankee whose grandparents came over here from Bristol, England, in 1635, and I was brought up that way."

Raised in a Congregational church, Millett also believes that faith in God is an important part of America's historic destiny. For a while, he even served as a part-time preacher.

"My family didn't go to church that much, but I used to go every Sunday and to Wednesday prayer meetings," he says. "I became interested in the faith and was baptized when I was a senior in high school.

"I preached at some churches when I was attending Bates College in Lewiston, Maine. I felt people needed an awareness of where we come from and where we're going. But I never really felt called to be a full-time pastor."

Instead, Millett felt a powerful calling to fight in Europe in World

War II. Ironically the fact that he felt that calling before America officially entered the war led this true-blue Yankee to desert the U.S. Army and volunteer with the Canadian forces.

FROM DESERTER TO WAR HERO

America didn't enter the war until 1941, but Germany had been indicating it might attack France since at least 1936, and soon after attacked Austria, Czechoslovakia, and Poland.

In 1940, Private First Class Lewis Millett enlisted in the Army Air Corps, training as an air gunner. But he was impatient for American forces to join the fray. When it became increasingly clear that wouldn't happen, he deserted and joined the Canadian army.

"Basically it goes back to this," he says. "Why is it that we are a free and independent country? It's because men believed deeply in that idea of freedom and fought for that. I believe as a free man, it is my duty to help those who are subject to tyranny.

"When President Roosevelt said we were not going to fight, and no American boy was going to die on foreign soil, I said to heck with that. I'm going to go join the Canadian army."

For his actions, Millett was court-martialed and fined fifty-two dollars, making him the only Medal of Honor recipient to have received such a punishment.

But after America joined the war, Millett was welcomed back and made second lieutenant, serving in the First Armored Division. Within weeks of rejoining the American forces, he was fighting in North Africa, where he received the first of his many military medals: the Silver Star. Later in the war he received a Bronze Star.

"When it was all over, my unit had the longest combat record of anyone in World War II, six hundred days in both Africa and Italy," he says. "I've seen it all, and I fought with some very good units."

Throughout his time in World War II, Millett survived through a combination of unshakable confidence and deep faith in God.

"I'm arrogant," he freely admits, "and I honestly believe that it is not so much courage, but being arrogant that makes you 'courageous.' I didn't believe any enemy could kill me. If you're arrogant like I am, you have no fear, and you know no stupid Commie or Nazi is going to be able to kill you. Every time I was hit, I was surprised.

"Plus, I believe the good Lord looks after those stupid people like me. Before you go into a situation, you assume the good Lord's going to help you. And when you survive, you give thanks. I don't remember actually praying during combat. You're too busy doing your job and listening to all the people shooting at you. And it never actually crossed my mind that I might not survive. Nope. Never. And here I am over eighty years old and still going strong. Fear comes because people are afraid they're going to die."

Millett still believes his experiences in World War II shaped him and molded him in ways that had a profound impact on the rest of his military career.

"I grew up from a young person who didn't have any responsibilities in the world to someone at the end of the war who was a first lieutenant and was running a lot of things and doing a lot of things," he asserts. "During the war, I realized I had the capability of doing more than I could before."

BRAVERY IN KOREA AND VIETNAM

Millett didn't lay down his rifle when World War II ended. Instead, he joined the 103rd Infantry, Maine National Guard. He served with the 103rd for four years before joining the Eighth Field Artillery Battalion of the Twenty-seventh Infantry Regiment "Wolfhounds" in Japan.

Deployed to Korea, he was the commander of Easy Company when he led a bayonet charge against heavily fortified enemy positions, for which he received the Medal of Honor. The official award citation summarized his heroic actions:

Capt. Millett distinguished himself by conspicuous gallantry and intrepidity above and beyond the call of duty in action. While personally leading his company in an attack against a strongly held position he noted that the 1st Platoon was pinned down by small-arms, automatic, and antitank fire. Capt. Millett ordered the 3d Platoon forward, placed himself at the head of the two platoons, and, with fixed bayonet, led the assault up the fire swept hill.

In the fierce charge Capt. Millett bayoneted two enemy soldiers and boldly continued on, throwing grenades, clubbing and bayoneting the enemy, while urging his men forward by shouting encouragement. Despite vicious opposing fire, the whirlwind hand-to-hand assault carried to the crest of the hill.

His dauntless leadership and personal courage so inspired his men that they stormed into the hostile position and used their bayonets with such lethal effect that the enemy fled in wild disorder. During this fierce onslaught Capt. Millett was wounded by grenade fragments but refused evacuation until the objective was taken and firmly secured.

The superb leadership, conspicuous courage, and consummate devotion to duty demonstrated by Capt. Millett were directly responsible for the successful accomplishment of a hazardous mission and reflect the highest credit on himself and the heroic traditions of the military service.

Thinking back on that day on Bayonet Hill, Millett concludes that his family heritage helped inspire him to risk his life in defense of his country.

"The only reason I did that is because I thought of my grandfathers who fought in the Civil War. The man I was named after, Lewis Morton, my great-grandfather, had fought in the Civil War in the Fourteenth Maine regiment. I knew he had done bayonet assaults."

Millett's bravery encouraged his men, who killed forty-seven of the enemy, eighteen of them dying from bayonet wounds.

"I'm alive because the men I was leading believed in me and did what I asked them to do. They deserve the Medal of Honor as much as I do."

Vietnam was a much different war, and America was a much different place in the 1960s than it was in the 1950s. Still, Millett served in a supporting role to the Vietnamese fighting forces because he believed that they, too, deserved the kind of freedom many Americans took for granted.

"Unlike some dirty and despicable politicians, I believed that Asian people deserved the same freedoms we have," says Millett, who was promoted to colonel in September 1967.

"We are the only country in the world that sends soldiers to fight for other people throughout the world and gives them their freedom. American soldiers have gone and fought and bled and died in state after state, from Tunisia to Algeria to Morocco. And in all of these, we made them free. We didn't convert them into American colonies. This is a tribute to the meaning of the United States of America."

Millett received his own tributes in Vietnam, but he decided to decline any further U.S. medals.

"I wasn't over there to get decorations," he declares.

LOSS AND REMEMBRANCE

In the 1980s American forces were a part of the multinational peacekeeping force in the Sinai. And like his forefathers had done, Millett's youngest son, John, volunteered to serve.

Staff Sergeant John Millett, twenty-four other U.S. soldiers, and eight crew members were killed on December 12, 1985, when their transport plane exploded in Gander, Newfoundland.

"He called me before he volunteered," says Millett. "He said they needed medical men in Sinai. I told him we always volunteer. I wish I hadn't, but it wouldn't have been true to the meaning of our lives to do otherwise.

"He was my youngest son at twenty-seven years old. I had just talked to him on the phone the day before as he was leaving Germany. When the news came on TV that an aircraft from Germany had crashed in Canada, we knew immediately he was there. The tragedy just killed my wife. She had a heart attack, from which she never recovered."

In the troubled days and weeks after the disaster, Millett wondered what God had to do with his son's death.

"Why do some die while others don't? If you're a believer, it's difficult to accept that God allows something like that to occur. But that's why He gave us freedom of choice. It is our choice, and it is also our enemies' choice."

In his grief Millett began writing down the words of a simple prayer. "I did it about two weeks after John was killed," he explains. "Actually it came out rather easily."

Now, when Millett speaks at veterans' events, he recites the lines, which he calls "An Old Soldier's Prayer":

> I have fought when others feared to serve.
> I have gone where others failed to go.
> I've lost friends in war and strife,
> Who valued Duty more than love of life.
>
> I have shared the comradeship of pain.
> I have searched the lands for men that we have lost.
> I have sons who served this land of liberty,
> Who would fight to see that other stricken lands are free.

I've seen the weak forsake humanity.

I have heard the traitors praise our enemy.

I've seen challenged men become ever bolder,

I've seen the Duty, Honor, Sacrifice of the Soldier.

Now I understand the meaning of our lives,

The loss of comrades not so very long ago.

So to you who've answered duty's siren call,

May God bless you, my son. May God bless you all.

A Son Remembers a POW

Millett's older son, Lewis Millett Jr., or Lee, also served his country's armed forces, inspired in part by the bravery of his dad.

"He made Rambo look like Captain Kangaroo," says Lee.

Once he returned to civilian life, Lee turned his attention to creating beautiful works of sculpture. One of his works pays honor to Air Force Captain Lance Sijan, the Medal of Honor recipient who was captured and imprisoned by the North Vietnamese. During his imprisonment, Sijan refused to divulge information to his captors, and he made repeated attempts to escape.

Those defiant efforts led to his torture, which ended in his death, and then to his fame among servicemen who believe Sijan's determined defiance represents the courage and commitment that characterize America's fighting forces at their best.

The rugged bronze sculpture shows Sijan kneeling in his cell, looking to the heavens. According to Lee, this is an acknowledgment of the reality of God's presence at life's most trying times.

"The only One who is really with us when we are born or when we die is God," says Lee, who spent hours trying to get the airman's facial details correct in order to bring home the humanity of the thousands of POWs who have died on foreign soil.

"They weren't anonymous," notes Lee. "They all had faces and names and hopes and dreams."

The sculpture also features a prayer that is written on the ground in front of the kneeling Sijan. This "Prayer of the POW" reflects Lee's belief that God was there for Sijan at a time when his fellow countrymen were unable to rescue him:

> I look not to the ground
> For I have no shame
> I look not to the horizon
> For they never came
> I look to God.
> I look to God.
> God bless America.

PARADES AND PATRIOTISM

As a decorated war veteran and full-throttle patriot, Lewis Millett Sr. has participated in hundreds of parades and memorial services for American soldiers. One of the most dizzying was the 1951 Tournament of Roses Parade in California.

"I was one of the grand marshals," he recalls. "I didn't realize at the time that there were thousands and thousands of people along the route, but with all those people waving, it was like I was at sea. I felt like I was seasick."

Since the terrorist attacks on America on September 11, 2001, even more Americans have been turning out at patriotic parades and rallies.

True to form, Millett still participates in as many of these as his daughter-in-law Amy can ferry him to and his old soldier's body can accommodate.

"Sometimes I feel like I'm going to live forever, but not when I try to get up and walk," he says. "It's amazing how I've abused the body, paratrooping into places, engaging in hand-to-hand combat demonstrations where I would kick people and have people kick me back in the stomach.

"You shouldn't be doing things like that to the human body, and I have to watch it now because I can't punch out people like I used to."

But he can still deliver rousing, emotional speeches about America's values and heritage.

Veterans Day 2001 found him involved in three separate activities: a ceremony at Riverside National Cemetery in Riverside, California, an event at the Air Museum in Palm Springs, and a later Palm Springs parade.

Millett was surprised by the turnout at all of the events, and he sees the resurgence of patriotism after the September 11 attacks as proof of Americans' commitment to the country's core values.

"I was told that there were more people there in Palm Springs than at any parade they had had before," he says. "It goes to show that if we're attacked and people realize what's at stake, we will come together.

"In recent years we have become fat and comfortable as a country because we have faced no major pressures. At these times, the idea of patriotism kind of goes away. But when we're under pressure, it comes back. And I believe it will last."

He is particularly encouraged to see so many fellow citizens waving the American flag, a symbol that fell into some disrespect in recent decades.

"It burns my soul when someone burns the flag or takes the art of the flag to make a shirt or something like that. The flag has a deeper meaning to me than mere wearing apparel.

"My forefathers fought for this country. We fought in every war, and there's no other country like ours. I've lost so many friends fighting in foreign lands that anybody who dislikes America better not come to my house," Millett firmly states.

Listening to Millett talk, one can at times hear that the young man who preached in churches when he had the chance during his college days is still alive and well.

If he had a chance to preach a sermon today, he says it would focus on the themes of duty and responsibility.

"These are things that are endowed to us by our Creator," he argues. "Belief in duty and responsibility has eroded to some degree, but we're still the greatest country in the world because of these values."

Glad to be alive. *Captain Lewis Millett smiles for a photographer from* Stars and Stripes *magazine on February 7, 1951, the day led Easy Company's courageous bayonet assault on heavily fortified enemy positions in Korea. The photo was used to promote U.S. War Bonds in a series of ads appearing in major magazines, such as the* Saturday Evening Post.

Honored for his courage. *U.S. President Harry S. Truman (far right) congratulates Millett during the White House ceremony where Millett received his Medal of Honor on July 5, 1951.*

Patriotic evangelist. *Though he is over eighty, Millett still speaks to civic and military groups whenever he can. He often closes his rousing speeches with "An Old Soldier's Prayer," which he wrote after the death of his son John, who was killed in the line of duty in 1985.*

★ SEVEN ★

SHERM CONNOLLY

TOUGH AND TENDER

When most people think about the many Americans who served in World War II, they naturally think about the men. That's understandable because most of the millions who served were the male soldiers and sailors who fought gallantly on the front lines. But behind the front lines, thousands and thousands of women served, too, doing their part to support the war effort.

Sherm Connolly was one of the first women to sign up when America launched the Women's Auxiliary Army Corps in 1942. Twenty-eight years later, when she finally retired from the army, she was a lieutenant colonel.

Today as eighty-four-year-old Connolly reflects on her action in World War II, she is thankful she had an opportunity to serve, and grateful for the changes the war brought to her life.

"I matured during that time," she says. "All of a sudden I realized that I could go places and do things. I developed a self-confidence I had never had before."

That self-confidence is evident to anyone who meets Connolly, an energetic woman who has continued to stretch herself and contribute to the lives of others.

DUST STORMS AND DEPRESSION

Sherm Connolly was born in 1918 in a sod house in remote Valentine, Nebraska, a town of three thousand souls. Her family soon relocated to the slightly larger town of Chadron in the Nebraska panhandle. Her given name was Iona Sherman, but by the time she was in elementary school, people began calling her Sherm, and the name stuck. Connolly came from her husband, James, who died in 1972.

Her youth was shaped by two major events of the 1930s: the Dust Bowl and the Great Depression. Times were tough, and Connolly learned to be tough too.

"It was a rough childhood," she recalls. "The dust storms coming across the prairie were so bad that if we drove outside of our little town of five thousand people, it would look like we were in a terrible snowstorm.

"The drifting would be deep. And here or there would be the feet of a cow or a horse sticking up out of drifting dirt. Farm equipment would be buried too. Occasionally you would see a mound of dirt with a steering wheel sticking out of the top. That was a buried tractor.

"People gave up housekeeping, due to all the dust that would come in through the doors and windowsills. Everyone lived in their kitchens, bathrooms, bedrooms. When the storm died down, they cleaned the dust from the rest of their houses with scoop shovels and brooms.

"I also remember the sky being a dirty brown color that was unbelievable. To make things worse, the summer temperature could reach one hundred and twenty degrees."

Connolly's grandfather had been in the army in Nebraska, and when he got out, he homesteaded on a nearby patch of land. There wasn't a tree in sight, and home building materials had to come across the vast prairie by train and then be transported to the homestead by horse-drawn carriage. So he chose to build a house of the native sod.

Her father, Abraham M. Sherman, worked as a farmer and lived in the same sod house. Connolly's mother, Viola Elliot, lived on the adjoining property with her sister. The two soon met and married.

Connolly was born on July 5, 1918. "I should have arrived on the fourth," she says, "but I was late then, and I have been late ever since."

In an effort to improve her lot in life, she attended a teachers' college, but she still seemed destined to spend the rest of her life in Chadron. Then World War II broke out.

"On the morning of December 7, 1941, I was teaching Sunday school to a class of girls at the Congregational church. We came home from church, turned on the radio, and heard the news of the attack on Pearl Harbor. It was shocking. In fact, it was just about as unbelievable as the tragic attack on America on September 11, 2001."

WOMEN AND WAR

America was at war, and the services of women were suddenly required in the U.S. war effort.

Women had plenty to contribute, and in time, tens of thousands of them would enter the workforce. They took the places of male workers who had been sent off to war. In factories across the country, the pioneering women made the equipment and ammunition the servicemen used. By 1943, women made up as much as one-third of the U.S. workforce.

When it came to waging war, though, most Americans believed that was men's work. Women had nursed soldiers in World War I. But even after Amelia Earhart flew solo across the Atlantic, many people remained convinced that women should focus on domestic duties.

Those ideas would change as World War II grew in scope, and a mind-boggling number of U.S. soldiers were sent to fight in Europe, Asia, and Africa.

England and the USSR went farther than other countries to utilize the resources their women offered. All unmarried British women between the ages of seventeen and forty-five were conscripted into auxiliary forces or worked in various support capacities. In all, hundreds of thousands of women contributed to the British war effort. And in the Soviet Union, women fought as snipers and regular combat forces on the war's vast Eastern front.

But in the U.S., traditional attitudes about women's place in life hindered their significant involvement, at least until 1942. After heated debate, Congress approved the formation of the Women's Auxiliary Army Corps (WAAC).

Connolly, who was anxious to participate in the war effort, was one of the first to sign up. "The Corps came along, and it was the answer to my needs and prayers," she says.

"I went to the recruiting station in Omaha, and the recruiter said, 'Why in the world do you want to join the army?' That was the attitude many people had."

She and other members of the WAAC who went to Fort Des Moines in Iowa were tried and tested.

"Fort Des Moines was a former cavalry fort," recalls Connolly. "The veteran soldiers from the old days of hard driving, hard riding, and hard fighting were our initial officers and cadre. When some of these soldiers saw us arrive for training, they said, 'We'll give this foolishness six weeks!'"

The women not only survived the training, but went on to impress some of their crusty trainers.

Next, Connolly went to Daytona Beach, Florida, and Fort Oglethorpe, Georgia, to train new recruits at two new WAAC centers. Then in the summer of 1943, the WAAC became the WAC as the word *Auxiliary* was dropped and the Women's Army Corps was born.

"We were really in the army now!" exclaims Connolly, recalling the excitement of those days.

"Before this, we had been authorized to serve with the army, not to be in it," she states. "Now we were full members of the wartime army, complete with all the responsibilities and benefits, including pay that was equal to that of men, and later access to the GI Bill."

OVER THERE

Women who had joined the WAAC weren't required to remain in the WAC, but most did, exhibiting the same kind of patriotism and dedication that had spurred American men to join the war effort.

"War was on," recalls Connolly. "We were ready for anything that would win the war. The depth of patriotism and love of country that we experienced early in 1942 was not repeated until the tragic terrorist attack of September 11, 2001, shocked the nation."

Connolly finished Officer Candidate School and received a commission as a second lieutenant. Her first assignment was in the Pentagon, where she worked in the office of the chief of ordnance. Then in early 1944 she shipped out to England, where she worked to supply U.S. soldiers with the equipment needed for the D-Day invasion.

"Immediately before D-Day, General Dwight Eisenhower issued an order that the troops would be supplied with all the major items like tanks, trucks, guns, and heavy equipment," she says. "We worked day and night, slept for three or four hours, then went back and worked some more."

She can still recall surveying the vast ordnance depots: "England is known for its rolling hills, and the U.S. depots covered those hills as far as eyes could see. It's a wonder that little island didn't sink underneath the weight of all that equipment."

Her next assignment was France, where she helped get supplies to soldiers in the country in the days and weeks after the Normandy invasion.

The work was demanding, and the living conditions in Normandy were rough, but Connolly had never been more excited about life. At the same time, seeing injured and dead soldiers reminded her that life was precious.

Perhaps it's not surprising that during that time Connolly experienced a deepening of the Christian faith she had loosely embraced as a child.

"Throughout the years, I had a yearning for something more," she says. "I believe the first time I realized this was during an Easter service led by an army chaplain under the Eiffel Tower. He told stories about the war and taught about the resurrection from the dead. There wasn't a dry eye there."

Over the following years, military chaplains—many of them Catholic—would have a profound impact on Connolly's life.

"I grew up in an area where anti-Catholic feelings were pretty strong. Still, I married a Catholic, so I can't say those feelings influenced me.

"And even though I never fully embraced the Catholic faith, I appreciated the formality and ritual of Catholic worship and felt it showed a formal respect that is due a higher power."

Connolly's interest in the sacred grew more intense as she enjoyed the opportunity of visiting some of Europe's major cathedrals. The beauty and the majesty of these sites still stir her emotions and inspire her to reflect on the grandeur of God. Her yearning for spiritual fulfillment would continue throughout her military service, but only after her retirement would she act on it. At the age of fifty-three, she was baptized and confirmed in the Episcopal Church.

BEYOND GENDER STEREOTYPES

After the war was over, Connolly returned to Nebraska, but the opportunities for women there weren't as exciting as the work she had done for the past three years.

In 1948, President Harry S. Truman signed the Women's Armed Services Act, which gave women the privilege of serving in all branches of the military. As a result, even more women entered the U.S. armed forces, and Connolly returned to active duty as a commander of a WAC basic training company at Fort Lee, Virginia.

During the Korean War, she commanded a large WAC detachment in Tokyo.

After the Korean War, she was assigned to Chicago, where she served as the WAC's chief of recruiting, overseeing the work of twelve recruiting centers in thirteen states. And in the 1960s, she was the officer in charge of a WAC exhibit team that toured the country under the title "Serving with Pride and Dignity." The team educated Americans about the important military roles that women had played from the time of the Revolutionary War to the present.

Today, women have far greater opportunities than Connolly did. And some of the pioneering members of the contemporary women's movement rightfully look back at women in the WAC as their proud predecessors.

Connolly thinks women can do "just about everything" men can, and she certainly supports the rights of women to earn equal pay for equal work. Yet she's no feminist, and she has deep misgivings about many of the directions the women's movement has taken.

"I think they've gone too far," she says. "There's a line of demarcation between men and women and a respect for women that has been lost. I support the advancement of women in their careers and work, but the burning of bras and the free sex of the 1960s went too far.

"Perhaps in some ways I'm a pretty straitlaced Victorian-type woman. I believe that sex is the greatest gift God gave us, but it was intended for marriage. Part of the problem with some of the social changes of the last few decades is that many of our moral standards went out the window."

Even during the height of her war work, Connolly maintained an attractiveness and femininity, and the men she worked with treated her with respect and opened doors for her. She misses some of these social conventions and the traditional understandings of gender distinctions that supported them.

When she wants a model for what women can be, she looks not to the feminists of the last third of the twentieth century, but to her mother, who combined toughness and tenderness during some terribly difficult decades.

"My mother was probably the prettiest and most feminine woman you ever saw," she says. "She wanted to have a nice home and to set a beautiful table for dinner. Of course, she never got all of that in Dust Bowl Nebraska, but that was her aim."

Connolly also believes that women's strength is found in service, not in a self-centered emphasis on personal rights. And she has continued to serve others throughout her postmilitary years.

She was the only female member of the committee that helped found Liberty Heights, the retirement complex in Colorado Springs where she now lives. But she is far from retiring, and she regularly recruits fellow residents to get involved in community activities.

"In Japan elderly people are revered," she says. "But here in America, we warehouse them, and for many retired people, their greatness is all in their past. That's too bad."

Connolly still has work to do, though. She has served on the advisory council of the local Salvation Army, is a member of the local Rotary Club, and volunteered with the Assistance League, a women's group that provides clothing and medical assistance for low-income families and children.

"You've got to give something in this world," she says. "If you don't, what good are you?"

Proud to serve. *After enlisting in the Women's Auxiliary Army Corps and serving as an officer in the Women's Army Corps, Sherm Connolly was the officer in charge of a WAC exhibit team that toured the country under the title "Serving with Pride and Dignity." She is shown here in the team's unique uniform.*

EIGHT

WILLIAM NESBITT

FINDING REDEMPTION AFTER FAILURE

To most people, William Nesbitt would qualify as a bona fide hero. What else can one call a person who throughout his life has repeatedly risked everything to help others?

He even has World War II medals to support the claim, including a Presidential Unit Citation awarded to him and other members of the Seventh Naval Beach Battalion for dedication to duty under unusual circumstances on Omaha Beach during the D-Day invasion of Normandy.

But Nesbitt, a humble and self-effacing man in his upper eighties, isn't so sure that such a lofty term as *hero* should be applied to someone like him.

"I was no more a hero than the farmer raising wheat, the housewife welding ships or the laborer digging ditches," says Nesbitt, a former practicing doctor and freelance writer, in an article he wrote for *Physician* magazine, published by Focus on the Family.

"I didn't choose to go into one of the bloodiest battles that the world has ever seen; I was given orders to go. And like any officer or sailor, I obeyed my orders and did my duty to the best of my ability."

As a writer, Nesbitt pays close attention to words and their meanings, and he thinks the word *hero* is often applied too liberally.

"There were heroes on Omaha Beach that bleak, cold day," he writes. "Like the Army sergeant who strapped 70 pounds of plastic explosives on his back and ran through 50 yards of intense enemy fire to blow a hole in a seawall that was blocking the advance of our tanks and troops.

"And the senior medical officer who was declared missing in action when his ship was sunk by an artillery shell. Uninjured and fit for duty, he appeared on the beach two days later, ready to serve."

Nesbitt was a medical officer, and his duty on that blood-stained beach was to provide temporary care for the wounded and prepare them for evacuation to military hospitals in England. It's a duty he carried out with care and devotion, dodging enemy bullets and mortar fire as he sought out and bandaged injured soldiers.

It's been more than half a century since D-Day, but Nesbitt still thinks back on the events on Omaha Beach with a mixture of sadness and regret. Even though he did more than might have been expected, he felt he had done less than he should.

A descendant of a long line of military men, medical doctors, and ministers, Nesbitt fears that he gave too little attention to the spiritual and emotional needs of the men he was attending.

"The vision of hundreds of casualties lying quietly in rows, lonely, in pain, silently pleading for someone to comfort them, lingers in my mind," he writes.

"If only I had seen the need to go down those rows and kneel beside each man, say a prayer, offer an encouraging word, take a message for a loved one."

Some may think that Nesbitt is being a bit too hard on himself, but his regret led to soul-searching and a reevaluation of his priorities. And in the long run, his experiences on the beaches of Normandy would transform his postwar life, changing the way he would relate to people for decades.

FIRST BRUSHES WITH DEATH

For many of the young men fighting in World War II, Normandy provided their first encounters with the reality of death.

But not William Nesbitt. The first times he met the Grim Reaper up close came during the depths of the Depression, when he was a troublemaking teenager. One of his close calls came during a cold, snowy winter evening in 1929 as a fifteen-year-old. Nesbitt and a buddy named Gordon were selling Christmas trees in depression-era Baltimore.

Sales were slow that night, and Nesbitt wondered what it would be like to take a ride on his sled, which was leaning up against a fence. He looked at the five-block-long hill that stretched out before him, its intersections marked by the warm glow of gas street lamps. It presented an irresistible picture.

Gordon turned this temptation into action. He grabbed his sled, ran half a dozen steps down the hill, and belly-flopped onto its surface. Gliding rapidly down the hill, he was surprised when Nesbitt jumped on top of him, the extra weight adding to the sled's speed.

The pair darted through one gas-lit intersection, and then the second. As they flew through the third intersection, a taxicab turned onto the hill and began following them.

Nesbitt was certain that the taxi driver would be able to see him, but he wasn't so lucky. The front wheel of the cab struck the sled, running over both of Nesbitt's legs and sending Gordon sprawling in the snow and ice.

Surprisingly Nesbitt survived the accident. He was hospitalized for six weeks as doctors performed reconstructive surgery on his legs.

D-Day Heroes Finally
Get Their Memorial

Approximately twenty-five hundred American and Allied soldiers died on June 6, 1944. It took sixty-seven years for the residents of Bedford, Virginia, to have a memorial honoring their service.

On June 6, 2001, President George W. Bush traveled to Bedford to dedicate the new National D-Day Memorial. The major D-Day Museum is in New Orleans.

Instead of being erected near the Mall in Washington, which is already the location of so many national monuments, the D-Day memorial was erected in this small town, which had lost so many of its young men on that fateful day.

Upon this beautiful town fell the heaviest share of American losses on D-Day, said the president as he stood before the memorial, which includes a towering granite arch inscribed with the word *Overlord,* which was the military name of the massive operation.

The memorial also features granite representations of a landing craft opening its door to a large reflecting pool and a number of soldiers.

One of the men in the sculpture is dead, but others are making their way out of the water, across the beach, and up the adjoining cliff.

Bedford was the home of thirty-five of the soldiers who took part in the invasion. Nineteen of these young men died during the first fifteen minutes of the operation, and two more died later that same day.

In the audience that day were veterans as well as family members who came to remember the losses of those like the Bedford boys, who were buried in French graves. Tears came to many eyes as the president described a generation of young men and women who, on a date certain, gathered and advanced as one, and changed the course of history.

Early in 1930, he came even closer to death. The sledding accident had worsened a heart condition that had kept Nesbitt home from school. His mother phoned the doctor to see what could be done.

Lying in his bed, Nesbitt quietly picked up an extension phone and listened in on the conversation. It was then that he heard the doctor utter these words: "There is nothing more that I can do. When the end comes, I'll sign the death certificate."

He hung up the receiver and prayed to God: "Dear Father, forgive me for the sins that I have committed. I love You. I'm Yours, all that I am, all that I have, all that I hope to be."

Nesbitt wrote about these experiences in *Decision* magazine, which is published by the Billy Graham Evangelistic Association. As he explained in the article, he wasn't begging for God's miraculous intervention.

"I didn't ask to be healed or to have my life spared," he wrote. "I asked God to put His arms around me and to hold me close. I sensed no assurance that I would live, but I could feel His love. I knew that He would be with me in life or in death.

"No longer afraid, I drifted into a peaceful sleep, not knowing if I would wake up."

A Surprising Recovery

Nesbitt did wake up, and over time his legs and his heart improved enough that he was able to return to school and achieve a lifelong dream. After completing medical school at Duke University, he enlisted in the navy.

"I had always wanted to be in the navy," he says. "My great-grandfather had been a privateer in the War of 1812. The navy was exactly what I wanted."

Due to an administrative mix-up, Nesbitt received two sets of orders simultaneously. One assigned him to convoy duty in the North Atlantic. The other assigned him to a beach battalion.

"I really didn't have a clue what that meant," recalls Nesbitt. "I figured it had something to do with amphibious landings.

"Also, I had a cousin who was six months older than me. He was also a navy doctor. He told me that convoy duty was about the worst thing you could ever experience. He said the seas were always rough, and you never got to port."

Nesbitt chose the beach battalion, and as soon as his battalion began its course of rigorous training, the consequences of his choice became much clearer.

"Part of the time we trained with members of elite troops like the Scouts and the Raiders," he says.

"We marched in loose sand with full packs that weighed forty to fifty pounds. We went out and climbed cargo nets on ships in rough seas. I even remember one time we were training in Maryland; we were doing amphibious training there. It was December or January, and it was so cold there was ice on our hair and clothing.

"Training was physically stressful, but since I had been a ninety-seven-pound weakling during high school, I was hyped up about building myself up."

The training would pay off once he reached the thick of battle. And so would his previous encounters with death and with God, which helped give him the inner strength and stability he needed to risk his security to care for men who lay wounded and bleeding there.

But true to his nature, Nesbitt declares that there was nothing unusual in that.

"In retrospect it can be said that people did make some unusual decisions," he allows, "but that went for everybody who landed on that beach."

CHAOS AND CARNAGE

June 6, 1944, began gray and overcast as the first waves of Allied assault troops hit the beaches of Normandy at 6:00 A.M. New waves of troops were scheduled to land every hour. Nesbitt's battalion was due on Omaha Beach at noon, but things didn't turn out as planned.

"Chaos reigned, schedules collapsed, command structures were shattered, and military units became fragmented and leaderless," he says.

Even before his landing ship had left England's Plymouth Harbor, there were problems. Ships crossing the Channel tried to protect themselves from enemy fighter plane attacks with barrage balloons—large, gas-filled balloons that were attached to the bows and sterns of the ships by 150-foot cables. Enemy pilots were afraid of having their planes become entangled in the cables, so when they attacked, they did so from some height.

The ship upon which Nesbitt and other soldiers were being transported hadn't been equipped with the balloons; it had to leave port without them. But a determined captain located two balloons and brought them to the ship in a small boat.

After the ship had crossed the Channel and was anchored a hundred yards off Omaha Beach, those balloons may have saved the soldiers' lives. A Nazi plane painted with U.S. markings, attempting to drop three bombs on the ship, did so from an angle. The bombs exploded in the water a few yards away from the hull, which caused their share of damage and fear on board.

The next problem they faced was the congestion on Omaha Beach. Men and machines had become bogged down and were unable to move at a normal pace. As a result, the beach battalion commander postponed further landings until the congestion decreased. Instead of hitting the beach at noon as planned, they waited in the turbulent waters overnight, landing at four o'clock the next morning.

As soon as he got close to the beach, Nesbitt understood better what had been causing the congestion.

"The scene was appalling," he says. "At the water's edge, body parts of our own troops floated, and corpses rolled in and out with the waves like logs. Hundreds of dead and dying were scattered over the vast stretches of beach. In fact, there were so many dead that their bodies obstructed the passage of heavy equipment and men trying to make their way inland."

Tank commanders, for example, wanted to cross the beach as quickly as they could, but they were slowed down because they didn't know whether the bodies on the beach were dead and alive.

"Their own humanitarian instincts slowed up some of the progress," reports Nesbitt.

A Foxhole Physician

Allied planes had bombed Normandy's beaches, but they hadn't routed out all the enemy troops. Once Nesbitt landed, his first assignment was to dig a foxhole for himself.

"I was scared," he says. "All of us were scared. When machine guns started shooting at you, you wanted to get out of the way. So we did the best we could.

"You were not going to be doing anyone else any good if you didn't have a place to shelter yourself. We were under machine-gun fire, sniper fire, and mortar fire the entire time. There was a cliff right behind the beach, and the German ground troops were still entrenched in bunkers and pillboxes right above the beach. It took about three days before all of that was cleaned out."

In the meantime Nesbitt cared for those he could reach, taking cover when the firing became too intense.

"It was triage," he recalls. "You sort out those cases you know are going to die, and you put your energy into caring for the rest.

"There were all kinds of problems, some of them psychological as well as medical. In situations like that, there are some rather severe mental cases that develop among people.

"Our main responsibility was not providing serious medical care. Rather, our job was providing immediate first aid and evacuating people. Army engineers had laid down a steel mat that planes used as a landing strip, so some of the more seriously wounded were evacuated by air.

"Others were evacuated by ship. The ones I put on the ships had fractures and other less life-threatening injuries that could wait twenty-four hours before they had better medical care."

Nesbitt's equipment was minimal.

"I had a tan canvas instrument case that contained a scalpel, scissors, hemostats, and a needle holder. We had lots of sutures, antiseptics, battle dressings, morphine, splints, plasma, and litters."

Darkness fell around 11:30 every night. In the morning German planes strafed the beach, trying to hit as many sleeping soldiers as they could.

"We were sleeping on that beach for three weeks," he says.

The days were grueling. Nesbitt and other medical officers raced from casualty to casualty, providing what superficial help they could before sending the men off to hospitals where they would receive more thorough care.

Many of the medical men joined the other soldiers in death during the long days of intense fighting. Nesbitt had his share of close calls, but they weren't what worried him. Rather, he felt regret over not giving each man more personal attention.

"The specter of that scene haunts me," he wrote.

I see long rows of wounded waiting to be evacuated. I remember my frantic effort to find transportation and how I agonized over the long delays in moving so many wounded.

Landing craft with their gaping bows sucked in dozens of wounded for transport back to England as Army medics whisked wounded off to a hastily constructed air strip.

I wouldn't have reached them all, but I would have brought love, hope and comfort to some.

A Prescription for Better Care

When you ask World War II veterans what kind of impact the war had on their later lives, many of these men speak in generalities. They talk about how it made them stronger or more mature, or how it tested their courage.

When you ask William Nesbitt what difference the war made, his answer is direct and precise: "When I came back and worked as a doctor, I put the lessons of D-Day into practice."

Working first with a partner in Richmond, California, and later as part of a medical group in Fairfield, Nesbitt practiced medicine in the way he hadn't been able to do when he was under fire: he spent time with each patient and did his best to treat each person as a unique individual.

He soon realized that civilian doctoring had at least one similarity to the triage he practiced at Normandy: many patients are troubled by a mix of physical and psychological ills. Nesbitt went to the University of

California at San Francisco for a course on psychiatry for family physicians, and he added as much psychotherapy to his medical sessions as possible.

"There were many people who thought there was a stigma attached to going to a psychiatrist to discuss their problems," he says. "When people came in to see me and I realized that some of them had really serious emotional differences, I concluded that they really needed help just as much as someone with a broken leg.

"Over the years, I would typically see these patients first in the morning and last in the afternoon so we could have more time together."

One of his most famous patients was baseball legend Ty Cobb. In twenty-two seasons with the Detroit Tigers, Cobb hit his way to the game's highest lifetime batting average (.367). But when he took off his cleats, Cobb had as many problems as many noncelebrities.

"On his initial visit to my office, I offered to pray with him," recalls Nesbitt. "That did more to help his needs than any medication I could have prescribed."

In addition, Nesbitt found plenty of ways to apply his faith outside the walls of his office. Between 1948 and 1953, he spent his days directing student health services at the University of Wyoming, but in his spare time he was the faculty sponsor for the university's InterVarsity Christian Fellowship program.

He later served as a national board member with Young Life, an international ministry working with young people, and during the height of California's hippie movement, he founded Youth Projects, an organization that worked with San Francisco–area teens and helped launch the Haight-Ashbury Free Medical Clinic, where Nesbitt worked as a doctor.

His war experiences had shown him that political and military conflict caused all manner of problems around the globe, so he helped found Refugees International, a group that worked with victims of such conflicts. He even went to Thailand to work personally with refugees in a Thai-Cambodian border camp.

And in 1978, he was named disaster medical coordinator for the state of California.

But the earthquake that shook up Nesbitt's life came in 1987, when he realized his wife, Bernice, had developed senile dementia. Even though some of his professional peers argued that Bernice should be institutionalized, Nesbitt resigned his other duties to devote all his time to being her primary caregiver.

Nesbitt is a firm believer in the sovereignty of God. As a result, he thinks the things that have happened to him are no accidents, but are opportunities for him to experience a deeper sense of God's love and grace.

As he focused all his care and attention on his wife and loved her through her agitation, delusions, and hallucinations, he had a unique chance to apply the lessons God had helped him learn on D-Day.

"In 1948 when I married Bernice, I loved her for her personal attributes and accomplishments," he says. "But now I realize those were selfish reasons. My feelings for her peaked recently when she was able to tell me how much she loved me.

"I then understood I loved her not for what she could give to me, but for the love and care I'm now able to return to her."

DOING THE WRITE THING

At a time in life when many other people would think about little more than their upcoming funeral arrangements, William Nesbitt has launched a new career as a freelance writer.

"I'm like a kid with a new toy," he says. "I have twenty-two topics in my computer just waiting to be developed."

In addition to writing articles for large-circulation magazines such as *Guideposts*, *Decision*, and *Focus on the Family*, Nesbitt has completed his first book, *The Illusion of Time: Seeing Science Through Scripture*. He is currently writing his second book, and its subject is forgiveness. One of its chapters covers a subject Nesbitt has had plenty of time to learn about since June 6, 1944: forgiving yourself.

NINE

JOHNNY WALKER

IMPRISONED NO MORE

Over the past eighty years, Johnny Walker has suffered so many tragic losses that he has learned to distinguish those things that are transient from those that are eternal.

Born in Little Rock, Arkansas, in 1922, Johnny was only five when he lost his mother to the worldwide influenza epidemic. When he was seventeen, his father died of a heart attack. Family members believe the death was at least in part caused by the rigors of surviving the Great Depression.

"We lost just about everything we had," recalls Walker. "A banker came out and took our cows, our mules, and our horse. Dad told the banker to leave the chickens alone, so we got to keep those."

Childhood on the farm was tough enough to prepare Walker for the trials he would face during his service in World War II.

"It was hard work," he says. "We dug up trees to prepare new ground for sorghum. When the sorghum plants matured every year, we would strip the leaves off and cut down the stalks for processing. One year, we had three hundred gallons of molasses.

"We also had cotton. I would pick the cotton, put it in a big sack, and drag the sack behind me to the next plant."

Without all the backbreaking work he had done on the farm, Walker doesn't think he would have survived the infamous Bataan Death March, which took the lives of some fourteen thousand American and Filipino soldiers. And without the toughness his Arkansas childhood had drilled into him, he doesn't think he would have made it through more than three years as a prisoner of war.

"We always went barefooted at home so I was used to it when I went three and a half years in prison camps with no shoes," he says. "I think the Lord had prepared me for some of the things I would go through."

But if the physical hardships Walker endured during the war were difficult, the spiritual struggles he would undergo once he got back home to America were equally challenging. These inner trials and tribulations would help him let go of the fleeting cares of this world so that he could tighten his grip on the things that would last for all eternity.

ALONE IN A BIG WORLD

Faith in God was something Walker learned from the time he was born. His parents were members of a church affiliated with the Assemblies of God, the largest of the new Pentecostal denominations to emerge from the Azusa Street Revival of the early 1900s.

Pentecostals dismissed the idea that God was distant and aloof. Instead they taught that God was nearby and ready to bless His people.

God was everywhere, of course, and His blessings fell on both the just and the unjust. But Walker's family believed that it wouldn't hurt their chances any if they attended services every time the church's doors were open.

"It seemed like we went to church every day," says Walker, who accepted Christ as his personal Savior when he was twelve years old. "I know we were there Sunday mornings, Sunday evenings, and Wednesday nights."

During those times when he wasn't at church, Walker learned to respect parental authority. "When Dad said no, he meant no," he recalls.

After his father died in 1940, Walker moved to Los Angeles to live with his brother Flay, who was attending Life Bible College, where he was studying to be a pastor.

Walker hoped to find a job, but times were still tough and work was hard to find. In February 1941 he enlisted in the Army Air Corps.

"I couldn't get a job in L.A.," he says. "I had always liked airplanes, and the recruiter told me there was one opening left in the Air Corps. I was thinking, *Hey, it's twenty-one dollars a month, and I would be around airplanes,* which is something I always wanted to do.

"I was eighteen years old, but I was small and didn't look that old, so Flay had to sign a form saying I was old enough to enlist. To me, it was just an adventure. I had no idea of what I was getting into."

After nine months of training, Walker was getting ready to ship out to Asia when he felt God tugging on his heart. He was attending church with his brother and his brother's wife at Angelus Temple.

The temple was the home base for evangelist Aimee Semple McPherson, one of the most flamboyant and controversial preachers of the twentieth century, and the founder of a new Pentecostal denomination called the International Church of the Foursquare Gospel.

As McPherson preached, Walker went forward to rededicate his life to Christ and receive baptism. His renewed sense of closeness to God would certainly come in handy in the coming months.

FIGHTING IN THE PHILIPPINES

In November 1941 Walker set sail for Pearl Harbor.

"Initially it was just a pleasant boat ride," he says, "but things changed once we hit Hawaii."

The Japanese attack on Pearl Harbor was still weeks away, but there was a tension in the air and a seriousness among the fighting men and their commanders that Walker hadn't witnessed before.

"The minute we left Pearl Harbor, we went into blackout mode. All curtains were pulled, all portholes were covered, there was no smoking on deck, and we were accompanied by two cruisers and two submarines as escorts. I knew this was not an exercise," he recalls.

Walker and the other men got to Manila eighteen days before the Japanese aerial attacks on Pearl Harbor and the Philippines. Stationed near Nichols Field, Walker experienced his first close brush with death during these bombing attacks.

"The morning of the attacks, I was lying on my bunk while a buddy was outside digging a foxhole," he remembers.

"My rest was interrupted by someone calling my name.

"'Johnny,' said the voice.

"I looked but didn't see anything.

"'Johnny,' cried out the voice again.

"Again, I looked around, but I still didn't see who was calling me.

"'Johnny,' said the voice a third time.

"I still didn't know what was happening, but the voice had gotten my attention.

"I walked over to my buddy who was digging the foxhole.

"'What do you want?' I asked.

"My buddy looked up, confused. 'I didn't call you,' he said.

"Just then, there was a tremendous explosion. I hit the ground. A second later, I was struck in the back. It was a chunk of dirt, but I was sure I had been hit by a part of the bomb.

"When the smoke cleared and I looked around, I saw that the bomb had landed on the spot where my bunk had been. The bunk, which was about thirty feet away, had disappeared. So had a water buffalo that had been standing about twenty feet away.

"If the voice hadn't called me three times, I would have been dead. This was just one of many times I felt the Lord's protection on my life."

Battling in Bataan

After the attack on Nichols Field, General Douglas MacArthur moved the U.S. and Filipino troops under his command to Bataan, a peninsula on the island of Luzon. He hoped that the troops could fight a delaying action until reinforcements arrived.

But as Walker recalls, the promised reinforcements never came.

"I was in the Thirty-fifth Air Group, the Twenty-first Pursuit Squadron, and my job was to take care of the machine guns on the P-40 Curtiss Warhawk, a single-seat fighter/bomber plane.

"When I wasn't working on the planes, I would be sent down to the front lines in a truck to deliver supplies and to pick up the wounded and the dead.

"I was a jack-of-all-trades and master of none. I knew we were in a war, and I could be the next man to die. Still, I had the feeling that the Lord was protecting me."

Once, when Walker was returning from the front lines with a truck full of corpses, he took a closer look, only to discover that one of the dead men held a live grenade in a death grip.

"The pin had been pulled," he says. "I used a pair of pliers and screwdriver to pry his fingers loose so I could get the grenade and throw it away before it went off."

In another case of divine intervention, Walker was preparing to get into an American-made truck when he felt a feeling that he should use another truck. He obeyed the feeling and got into an English-made truck that had the steering wheel on the right side of the passenger compartment instead of the left side, as is the case with American-made vehicles.

A few moments later, he was heading down a dirt road when enemy fire entered the left side of the truck. If he had been driving the American vehicle, he would have been killed in an instant.

Conditions in Bataan were horrible, and the soldiers were using World War I–era guns and grenades that often failed to work.

"We fought for four to five months with nothing," he explains. "We didn't have any supplies at all. The guns would jam. And the grenades we had would either not go off at all, or they would go off in the men's hands as soon as they removed the pins.

"They kept telling us that new supplies and reinforcements were on the way. But the supplies weren't getting there, and they were cutting our rations. So we knew something was going wrong."

On April 9, 1942, America surrendered its positions to the Japanese, and Walker and another seventy-five to eighty thousand men became prisoners of war.

"We didn't want to give up, but we had nothing to fight with," he says.

"The Japanese would have fought to the last man, and the American generals didn't want to waste all their men's lives. Commanding Officer Major General Edward King blamed himself for the surrender and asked us to forgive him. But we told him it was the only thing he could do."

Walker and the other men threw their guns and ammunition into a big pile in a rice paddy. Then they gathered at Mariveles Airfield, which they had been defending so bravely.

Then Japanese soldiers were in charge of the airfield, commanding them to fall into line and begin marching.

They didn't know it at the time, but the American and Filipino soldiers who started marching that day would keep marching for the next five days and five nights in a tragedy that historians would call one of the saddest events of a long and deadly war.

FAITH, HOPE, AND HATE

At first, Walker naively believed that the Japanese would treat their prisoners humanely. That belief was almost instantly destroyed.

"After we lined up, our captors began by stealing any valuables we had," he recalls. "Watches and pens were particularly popular, as they were small and easy to carry."

Some American alumni of West Point had their fingers chopped off so the Japanese could take their big class rings. And Japanese souvenirs were a special concern.

"Our captors believed that any Japanese souvenirs would have been taken from the body of a dead Japanese soldier, so they asked everyone to turn his pockets inside out."

Walker wasn't too worried about this command because his pockets were empty. Another American wasn't so lucky, however.

"Suspicious-looking coins fell out of the pocket of a young captain. One of the Japanese approached him, saying, 'You killed one of our men and took these coins from him.'

"'No, I did not get this from one of yours,' said the captain.

"'Yes, you did,' said the Japanese.

"Then, without any warning, the captain was forced down on his hands and knees. A Japanese sword was raised high in the air. It came down with a sickening sound. The captain's head fell to the dusty ground in a pool of blood.

"At that time, I knew we were in for a rough time."

Looking back on the war, Walker is convinced that that day more than half a century ago was when the hate began.

One of the most popular passages in the New Testament is found in 1 Corinthians 13. The passage uses beautiful language to describe the essence of Christian love, which is patient, kind, and keeps no record of wrongs.

The passage concludes with Paul's moving words: "And now these three remain: faith, hope and love. But the greatest of these is love."

This powerful passage was being turned upside down in Walker's mind. Starting the day the captain's head was cut off and continuing for the next three and a half years of imprisonment, he would survive in faith, hope, and hate.

"I had faith in the Lord, that He would give me strength," says Walker. "I had hope that I would be able to stand up and keep going for another day. And I had hate for the Japanese and everything they did to us."

Hatred would simmer in Walker's heart and course through his veins. Hate would keep him alert and watchful, and hate would keep him from striking back when Japanese guards harassed and beat him.

Hating went against everything Walker believed in, and he knew it was a dangerous feeling to give in to. But he also knew that only hate would enable him to survive the horrors of his imprisonment. He could deal with love once again when—and if—he ever got out of the living hell he inhabited.

THE LONG WALK

The march dragged on for more than sixty miles through some of the most rugged terrain the Philippines had to offer. April was one of the islands' hottest months, and the weather was dry in the period before the monsoon rains swept across the Pacific.

As the thousands of men marched, no one was permitted to stop for food or water. Those who did break ranks were shot or run through with a bayonet. As the march wound its way through hills and valleys, the soldiers walked past the decomposing bodies of dead comrades, some of them with limbs or heads chopped off.

Native Filipino families tried to throw food and water to the men, but some of the compassionate people were caught and executed, their bodies lying along the roadway with those of dead soldiers.

The men marched in rows of four, and when the Japanese weren't watching, they would bunch together and link arms, giving each other some support. Locking their elbows together as they marched, the men formed strong rows that enabled the two men in the middle to sleep while they walked as the two men on the outside kept the row moving and in proper order.

The men also talked to one another, encouraging one another not to break ranks in search of water or food.

"I didn't even know the names of the guys I was walking with, but we helped each other out," says Walker.

They went on and on, wearing through the soles of their shoes until they were walking barefoot over rough gravel and hot pavement. For the next three years, Walker would be barefoot, just as he had been back on the farm in Arkansas.

LIFE IN THE CAMPS

After five days and nights of walking, the captured soldiers arrived at San Fernando, where they were herded into cramped train cars. After a suffocating eight-hour ride, they were unloaded at Camp O'Donnell. Almost immediately it became clear that camp life would be even more brutal and inhumane than the forced march.

The Japanese commander who ruled the camp preached that whites were members of an inferior race—an idea whose truth was even more evident to him after the Americans had surrendered at Bataan instead of fighting to the death, as the Japanese soldiers were trained to do.

The camp held between fifty and sixty thousand men, but it had only two water faucets, which were turned on only a few hours each day. Those who were fortunate enough to fill their canteens while the water was on survived for another day. Those who missed out died of thirst.

"You would be sitting talking to someone," says Walker, "and without any warning, he would fall down dead."

Ironically the Japanese devised a devilish punishment for disobedient prisoners—water torture. Walker recalls seeing more than one man being bound and brought to an open place in the camp where all the dehydrated prisoners could see him. A water hose would be rammed down his throat, and the water would be turned on full force until the man's stomach exploded.

Walker's hatred for the Japanese captors grew by the day.

Then on May 6, 1942, an opportunity came to leave behind the insanity and death that surrounded him. The Japanese were looking for volunteers for a work detail. No details were given, but Walker knew it had to be better than the horrors of camp life. He thought he might even get more rations than the men at the camp.

He quickly volunteered, and soon he was helping 150 other men rebuild a wooden bridge that had been destroyed by American forces. The work was hard, the hours were long, the guards were cruel, and many men suffered from illness and disease.

Still, Walker knew that he would be more likely to survive if he was working instead of sitting around at a crowded camp. Plus the work provided an outlet for his hatred. In the crew of 150 men, each was given a number between 1 and 150, which was worn on a patch on the arm.

One night, Filipino guerrillas raided the old theater building where the work crew was sleeping. They had hoped to liberate the prisoners, but only one soldier left the theater with the guerrillas.

The next morning, the Japanese guards were irate.

"Some kind of punishment was forthcoming," recalls Walker. "At noon, a camp officer announced that he would shoot ten men. He said that he would shoot the five men on either side of the missing man's number."

Furiously the men started counting. Walker was shocked to discover that he was six positions away from the missing man.

The entire group of 149 men was taken to a hillside. There the ten men to be killed were pulled out of the group and shot. The remaining 139 men witnessed the executions at close range.

Once again, Walker's life had been spared. And day by day, the hatred grew.

Over the next three years, Walker would move rocks and pour cement to construct a gigantic Japanese airfield. (He and the other men tried to sabotage the project, but their one-thousand-foot-long airfield proved strong enough to hold hundreds of planes used by pilots training for kamikaze missions.)

"They walked right by us going to their planes," says Walker. "To see them preparing to go to their deaths for nothing was sad. I don't care if they were the enemy. I still had feelings for them. It was tragic just to see those kids' lives being wasted like that."

But Walker had little feeling for the guards who controlled their lives. One day, Walker took a momentary break from moving rocks so that he could stand up and stretch his back. As soon as he was upright, a guard hit him in the head with a shovel.

Meanwhile, family members back home in America were praying for Walker's safety. And they were regularly going to movies in order to see the newsreels that gave news about the war. They desperately hoped to catch a glimpse of Walker in one of the news shorts.

They never saw him in any of the newsreels, but Walker believes their prayers helped preserve his life through a series of close calls at various camps and on Japanese "hell ships." In addition to being subjected to unsanitary conditions on hot, cramped ships, the men were continually attacked by American planes, which didn't know the unmarked ships carried prisoners of war.

Walker's last assignment before liberation was to the Sendai POW camp in Hosokura, Honshu, Japan. An adjacent lead and zinc mine was owned by Mitsubishi, the Japanese industrial firm. There he worked in the mine using a pick and shovel to extract the valuable ore.

His testimony to the U.S. War Department's War Crimes Office detailed some of the punishment he and other men suffered at the camp. Daily food consisted of tiny amounts of grain and a thin, watery seaweed soup. About once a month, dog bones or rotten fish were added to the soup.

Malnutrition was commonplace, and men suffered from pellagra, scurvy, beriberi, defective eyesight, and emaciated conditions. Medical care was virtually nonexistent, many of the men were infested with fleas and lice, and frostbite was a common complaint.

Walker weighed only seventy pounds, so he wasn't able to work as much as he would have liked. Still, he was beaten by a guard for not being able to carry two long, heavy pieces of lumber.

"He struck me five blows with his right fist against my left ear," said Walker in his war crimes testimony. "The guard knocked me to the ground each time he struck me, that is, five times." The attack caused temporary deafness.

Walker also survived the collapse of the mines, helping a guard escape the ruined facility.

Then, one day, all the guards were gone, and soon they were replaced by American troops. The war was over. Liberation had begun.

HEALING THE HATRED

It would be many years before Walker was liberated from the hate he harbored toward the Japanese.

By war's end, Walker's brother Flay was the pastor of a Foursquare church in Ventura, California. Flay introduced Johnny to Carolyn Hardeman, a pretty young member of the church. Within six months, the two were married.

Walker loved Carolyn, but he still struggled with wartime horrors. Carolyn recalls those early years: "He was never mean to me, but you always felt that there was an undercurrent, and there was no way of knowing what would trigger him off.

"He had terrible dreams and nightmares. And one night, when we were camping out outside of Ventura, a tree popped and snapped during the middle of the night and began to fall over. This brought on a nightmare for Johnny, in which he found himself in the middle of a circle surrounded by a ring of Japanese soldiers shooting automatic weapons at him."

Walker got a daytime job at a hardware store, but the store was located only a few blocks from Little Tokyo, a thriving community of Japanese immigrants.

"If one of them had bumped into me, I would have tried to wipe him out."

Walker's various injuries and ailments led to an early retirement. In 1976 the couple bought a motor home, hoping to travel across the country and enjoy life together.

"We wanted to have fun like everyone else, but we absolutely dreaded it," says Carolyn. "We tried it for a year, but truly we both hated it. It seemed like such a waste of time and energy.

"We talked about it and decided to get rid of the motor home and find something more productive to do. That's what drew us to missions work and a group called Youth with a Mission [YWAM]."

CALLED BACK TO JAPAN

Johnny and Carolyn weren't youths any longer, but their desire to be involved in missions work was strong. So they enrolled in a YWAM training program in Hawaii called University of the Nations.

During the second day of their three-month training, a leader showed them a film of Christian work in Japan.

"That was our call," says Carolyn. "We looked at each other and agreed that this was what God intended for us."

Soon, the couple were in Japan, where Walker hoped that he would receive an apology from some of the Japanese for the way they had treated the Americans. Walker believed that if he got such an apology, he would be able to finally heal the hatred that had occupied his heart for so many years.

But that wasn't the way things would turn out. Instead, Carolyn received a message from God instructing the couple to forgive the Japanese, not the other way around.

"She woke me up and told me about the message," says Walker. "I said, 'No way am I going to do that.' But within a couple of days, God had spoken to me too. I realized I was going to have to forgive them."

The Walkers threw themselves into serving the Japanese people, helping them start and build new churches. After the work was done, they returned to Japan three more times to be with their newfound Japanese brothers and sisters.

Walker says they would go back to Japan again if it wasn't for his weak heart.

And he says he would enlist in the Army Air Corps again and serve his country, even if he knew that pain and imprisonment would follow.

"Yeah, I did it for my country, and I would do it again if I had to," he says. "Only this time I would know more about what to do to take care of myself better."

Walker thinks back on his war years, and instead of focusing on what was taken from him, he emphasizes what he received in the process.

"I think it made a better person of me," he states. "I was weak at home. I was small, the last of six children. The war made me stronger, and it showed me how to live and how to care for other people.

"It also drew me closer to the Lord. I realized that I have to depend on Him every day. Without Him, I can't do anything."

Honored after forty years. In 1985 Johnny Walker received a Bronze Star for the injuries he sustained while a prisoner at Japanese slave-labor camps.

Brotherly love. After the death of his father, Johnny Walker lived in Los Angeles with his brother Flay, who was studying to be a pastor. Flay was with Johnny at Angelus Temple when Aimee Semple McPherson preached. Johnny rededicated his life to Christ.

Pacific bound. Army Air Corps Sergeant Johnny Walker is shown before he sailed for Pearl Harbor.

No more nightmares. Johnny and Carolyn Walker have left the horrors of war behind and now focus on caring for their grandchildren and volunteering at their church.

TEN

REV. CHARLES CARROLL

WITNESS TO EVIL

Human beings are capable of both surprising goodness and shocking evil. Perhaps more than any other event in modern history, World War II powerfully illustrated the contrast between these two extremes of human nature.

It wasn't until the war was nearly over that people began to uncover the dim outlines of the most horrible of the Nazis' secrets. Their regime had created a killing machine that was as effective as it was faceless, and in more than a dozen concentration camps and death camps, some six million people—including millions of Jews and lesser numbers of Gypsies, homosexuals, and other "nonpersons"—were exterminated.

Winston Churchill said this Holocaust was "probably the greatest and most horrible crime ever committed in the history of the world." But how does one even begin to comprehend mass murder on such a grand scale, let alone compare it to other human tragedies?

People of faith believe that God can redeem any situation, and out of the evils of World War II at least one good thing did come. The atrocities conducted by the Germans were so damnable that in the years after the war, representatives of the United States, France, Great Britain, and the USSR organized the Nuremberg War Crimes tribunals, the world's first international criminal trials.

Thirteen separate trials were held between November 1945 and April 1949, each one focusing on a different group of alleged criminals—such as government leaders, diplomats, and industrialists—and a different set of crimes against humanity.

In 1947 Rev. Charles Carroll was an official observer of the so-called medical trial that focused on the gruesome "experiments" that members of the German medical profession conducted on unwitting victims, many of whom died torturous deaths.

Hundreds of people had probably been involved in wartime medical crimes, but only twenty-three were brought to trial. When the verdicts were rendered, some were sentenced to death by hanging, some were sentenced to prison, and others were acquitted.

Carroll never forgot about the things he had seen and heard at the trial, and he vowed to spend the rest of his life testifying to the evils that had been described in such excruciating detail.

This vow took him to the countries of France, England, Austria, and Switzerland where he conducted further research on the Holocaust. The vow also took him to Germany, Israel, and throughout the United States for a series of compelling lectures.

Some wondered why the pastor, who served in Presbyterian, Lutheran, and Episcopalian churches, spent so much time and energy on such a depressing topic. But for Carroll, to do otherwise would have represented a failure to fulfill a sacred calling: to serve as a witness to evil.

SEEING SIN FIRSTHAND

Carroll lived in Germany from 1937 to 1938 while studying at the University of Berlin. At that time, there were many people in Germany and elsewhere who didn't yet understand what Hitler was up to, but for Carroll, the signs were obvious as soon as he arrived in the country.

"I went to the American Embassy to inquire about finding a place to live," he said. "I had a very simple question: Do you know of an apartment near the university that I could rent at a reasonable price?"

The embassy employee who fielded the question startled Carroll when he asked, "Do you mind living with Jews?"

"Of course not," replied Carroll.

When he met his new landlord, a Hungarian Jew named Bernhard Marko, Carroll was surprised by the extensive preparations that had been made. Marko had installed plates of thick steel behind the beautiful panes of etched glass in the apartment's front doors, and he had stocked up on enough cyanide tablets to kill himself, his wife, and their daughter, Lilo, in case Gestapo agents managed to break through the reinforced doors.

"It will give Mother, Lilo, and me just enough time," said Marko.

Although Carroll had been naive when he arrived in Germany, he soon became wiser. And in the years since World War II ended, his extensive research into the Holocaust and his studies in world history have convinced him that human evil rarely emerges overnight. Rather, people usually succumb to evil step by step, act by act.

Carroll believes some of the most diabolical steps on the path to the Holocaust had been taken in the years before he came to Germany.

In 1933 the German legislature approved the Law for the Prevention of Congenitally Ill Progeny. Don't let the fancy title fool you. As journalist Tom Neven pointed out, it was a eugenics program that encouraged the increase of "racially healthy" Aryans, the Nazis' supposed master race of non-Jewish Caucasians, by practicing the "destruction of life unworthy to be lived."

In 1934 Germany amended its laws governing abortion. Before then, abortions were relatively rare, but after that time, a woman in even the late stages of pregnancy could be forcibly sterilized, which would result in the death of her unborn child.

By such means, Germany sought to purify the Aryan race by prohibiting "undesirables" from giving birth.

In the mid-1930s Hitler was still in the process of solidifying his hold on power. During those years, Germany's churches played a crucial role in the resistance movement.

"The chairman of the German Catholic Conference made it known to Hitler that they were unalterably opposed to the eugenics and abortion laws," says Carroll. "And these laws were defied by many Catholic physicians during the war."

This defiance was noted by Albert Einstein, who criticized other segments of German society for not opposing Hitler but praised the churches' role for standing up for the truth: "When the Nazis came to power I looked to the universities that prided themselves upon their intellectual freedom, and they failed me. I looked to the German press, which prided itself on the freedom of the press, and it failed me. Until at last the churches stood alone, and that for which I once had little regard earned my respect."

SUBVERTING HIPPOCRATES

Hippocrates lived from around 460 B.C. to 377 B.C. He was a Greek physician who is often regarded as the father of Western medicine. Although many of his procedures would seem primitive by the standards of contemporary high-tech medical care, the Hippocratic oath, which he wrote or possibly inspired, still serves as an ethical code for doctors worldwide.

A key portion of that oath, which was dedicated to the Greek god Apollo, reads as follows: "I will follow that method of treatment which, according to my ability and judgment, I consider for the benefit of my patients, and abstain from whatever is deleterious and mischievous. I will give no deadly medicine to anyone if asked, nor suggest such counsel; furthermore I will not give to a woman an instrument to produce abortion."

During the 1930s and 1940s, hundreds of German medical professionals violated this sacred oath. The twenty doctors and three medical assistants who were charged with conducting horrendous medical experiments at Nazi concentration camps were brought to justice in 1947 at the Nuremberg medical trial, which was officially known as *United States of America v. Karl Brandt et al.*

Nuremberg is one of Germany's most ancient cities, but much of its historic heritage was bombed to smithereens during World War II. After the war, the city played host to the historic war crimes trials that laid bare the details of some of the worst atrocities humans have ever committed on fellow humans.

Carroll was an official observer at the medical trial, where he heard horrifying accounts of the evils that doctors had performed on thousands of innocent victims.

Some doctors injected poison bullets into Russian prisoners and waited to see how long it would take for them to die. Others injected malaria and jaundice into Jews and Polish Catholics and took detailed notes on the results. There were also high-altitude experiments in which prisoners were subjected to simulated conditions similar to what would be experienced at altitudes of up to 68,000 feet, but without the benefit of oxygen. Other victims were placed in freezing water or subfreezing weather so that doctors could study their agonizing deaths.

Over the course of nineteen horrifying months, trial officials examined mounds of documentary evidence about experiments that killed thousands and left many survivors permanently disabled, physically or mentally or both. In addition, eighty-five victims who had survived the experiments testified about what they had endured and seen.

The doctors and assistants who stood accused of those deeds were Nazi Party members who had been recruited from Germany's finest medical schools and universities. Each one took the stand and attempted to mount a defense, but after a while, their comments began to sound all too similar. They were just following orders, they said. And after all, the government had sponsored and endorsed their activities. Who were they to stand in judgment?

"The trial gave me a traumatic shock," says Carroll. "We had no concept of radical evil then. We still don't today.

"Germany was in a moral vacuum. And moral vacuums, like natural vacuums, cry to be filled. Nazism filled this vacuum with a Darwinian ethic of 'survival of the fittest.' But this ethic could do little to protect those who were weakest or lacking in political power."

After the trials, Carroll had a conversation with a Jewish physician named Leo Alexander. Alexander explained why it was so easy for some doctors to subvert the Hippocratic oath and inflict so much pain and torture on their victims.

"Alexander told me that there is a difference between those who look upon their fellow human beings as common creatures of a common Creator and those who look upon them as a conglomerate of biologicals and chemicals."

TROUBLING PARALLELS

People throughout the world have condemned the deeds of some Germans during the 1930s and 1940s, but evil knows no geographical boundaries. Carroll believes other nations, including the United States, have also taken fateful steps in the direction of a reductionistic and amoral approach toward human life.

"Although you cannot identify a situation in the United States exactly like that of Nazi Germany, you can point to some parallels," he says.

Way back in 1927, the U.S. Supreme Court ruled in *Buck v. Bell* that involuntary sterilization was not unconstitutional. "They were sterilizing people in Virginia who they felt were incompetent—a large number of blacks, some poor whites," Carroll notes. The Nazis later cited this legal precedent when they provided a rationale for their own eugenics program.

Carroll points to other troubling medical studies, including the Tuskegee experiments of the 1930s. These U.S. government–sponsored procedures denied treatment to American blacks who were suffering from syphilis. And in the 1950s and 1960s, the Willowbrook experiments conducted on Staten Island used mildly retarded young people in hepatitis experiments.

Carroll is even more concerned about the millions of abortions that have been performed in America as well as efforts to legalize euthanasia.

In addition, countries like Sweden, Norway, Denmark, and Finland have, at various times, allowed involuntary sterilization.

"Such steps are evidence of the same moral vacuum I saw in Germany," says Carroll, who believes that our language reveals our moral relativity.

"A woman doesn't carry an unborn child today. She carries a fetus. A girl who in my time was promiscuous is today 'sexually active.'

"We have robbed everything of morality, and we have denied the child in the womb. As surely as we robbed the slave of his personhood and the Jew of his personhood, at the Nuremberg trials, we did it to the unborn child."

TESTIFYING TO THE TRUTH

God grants human beings so much free will that we can choose whether we want to live our lives doing acts of evil or spend the years we are granted sowing seeds of goodness.

God even grants us the right to ignore the truth, if we so choose, and when it comes to the Holocaust, there are some people who have chosen to turn their backs on the volumes of evidence generated by the Nuremberg trials. They claim that the horrors of the Holocaust were never committed. Some of these people speak of a widespread "Holo-Hoax."

In 1995 Rev. Charles Carroll spoke at a Holocaust memorial service that coincided with the fiftieth anniversary of the end of World War II and the liberation of the Nazi concentration camps. Although he didn't specifically mention the Holocaust deniers, he did add his own testimony to the evidence accumulated by so many others over the past decades.

"Not since the days of Moses had there been so systematic an attempt to eliminate one people from the face of the earth," said Carroll. "And this, with the benefits of a mighty army, a superb industrial, scientific, and technological complex, fortified by a barbarous terrorism."

In his comments Carroll challenged his listeners to add their voices to his: "Silence was then and is now a sin, and sin was then and is now more than a three-letter word in Holy Scripture. Can we reject the wisdom of John Donne, who said, 'Any man's death diminishes me, for I am involved in mankind'?

"The question remains, and upon our answer depends the future of civilization."

[Portions of this chapter are excerpted from profiles of Reverend Carroll that were published in *Citizen* and *Focus on the Family*, two magazines published by Focus on the Family.]

ELEVEN

CHUCK HOLSINGER

THE COURAGE TO FORGIVE

Three of the most powerful words ever uttered are, *Father, forgive them.*

Jesus had been crucified and was near death. As He hung on the cross between two common criminals, the Son of God had compassion on those who mocked Him, those who tormented Him, and those who sought to put Him to death.

The scene was a horrible one. Jesus was bruised and bleeding. Above His head hung a sign that read: "This is the king of the Jews." Some soldiers standing nearby jeered contemptuously: "He saved others; let Him save Himself." And at the foot of the cross, people cast lots for the privilege of dividing up His clothing.

But Jesus didn't respond in kind. Rather, the man who had spent the past three years teaching others about forgiveness used His last few breaths to exhibit divine love to His persecutors (Luke 23:32–38).

Of course, forgiveness had been a centerpiece of Jesus' preaching from the very beginning.

When His followers asked Him how they should pray, He instructed them to pray as follows: "Forgive us our debts, as we also have forgiven our debtors . . . For if you forgive men when they sin against you, your heavenly Father will also forgive you. But if you do not forgive men their sins, your Father will not forgive your sins" (Matt. 6:12–15).

On another occasion, Peter approached Jesus and asked, "Lord, how many times shall I forgive my brother when he sins against me? Up to seven times?"

Jesus' response is clear: "I tell you, not seven times, but seventy-seven times." Jesus then told Peter a parable about a poor man whose debts were forgiven by a king. But the poor man refused to show the same compassion to those who owed him money, and he was punished for his hardness of heart (Matt. 18:21–35).

Chuck Holsinger was a preacher's son from California who had heard sermons about forgiveness all his life. A Christian who believed that he had to live out his faith seven days a week for it to be authentic, Holsinger thought he understood what forgiveness required, and he attempted to practice it in his daily life. But war does strange things to people, forcing them to confront previously unimaginable horrors and reexamine their core values and beliefs.

When Army Private First Class Charles D. Holsinger shipped out to Asia, he confronted a Japanese enemy that practiced unspeakable atrocities with a single-minded devotion. And warfare itself seemed to demand a whole new understanding of Christian principles. Certainly God loves everyone. But soldiers can't show love to enemy fighters, can they? Rather, war seems to engender a seething hatred for the people on the other side. In part it's the hatred—but more than that, it's the struggle for survival—that inspires acts of battlefield gallantry, such as the brave acts that won Holsinger a Silver Star.

Even many years after the fires of battle had cooled, Holsinger harbored unshakable anger and hatred, which were expressed in disgust, disdain, and absolute distrust for the Japanese people and the products they manufactured and sold around the world. For years he was not comfortable riding in Japanese-made cars.

For Holsinger, the Japanese were to be shunned, just as Jesus' disciples had originally despised the Samaritans.

"I carried these feelings inside me," he says. "I just didn't want to have anything to do with the Japanese. I thought that was the best way to solve my anger. Maybe in that way I could in some way forget all about them. But in time, I came to see that I could never escape from these intense feelings."

It took a long time, but in the end, Holsinger repeated the powerful words of Jesus: "Father, forgive them." He also asked God to forgive him for wallowing in anger for so many years. And in the years he had left, he dedicated himself to doing everything he could to spread the message of Jesus' love and compassion to some of the very people who had been his enemies for so many years.

HEARING AND DOING

There have been ministers in the Holsinger family for three centuries. Members of the family helped found the Church of the Brethren in seventeenth-century America.

Chuck Holsinger's father carried on the tradition, serving first as a Presbyterian minister, but leaving that denomination in the 1930s as part of a movement opposed to growing theological liberalism within its ranks. Chuck's father served as the pastor of First Baptist Church in Salt Lake City during the worst of the Great Depression. Times were tough, and the family had no regular income. Instead, church members passed the offering basket and gave the Holsingers as much money as they could.

Meanwhile, Chuck and his older brother, Paul Jr., were getting into trouble.

"We would go up to the grocery store together. And while Paul would get the attention of the clerk, I would take things off shelves.

"One day, I was sitting in church on a Sunday morning. I was in the first grade. My father was preaching about sin. As he spoke, the Lord really convicted me about what I had been doing.

"That day when I came home from church, I talked to my father.

"'Why didn't you give an invitation? I wanted to become a Christian today.'

"He promised that he would give an invitation at the end of his sermon the next Sunday. I was the only person who went forward, but I confessed my sins and received Jesus as my Savior. The reality of the Lord's presence in my life was there right away."

In addition to growing up hearing about the love of God, Holsinger learned about love of country: "Loyalty to America was something my mother really emphasized."

And as the family lived year after year on offerings received from cash-strapped church members, Holsinger also learned the value of a dollar.

"Paul and I used to talk about the time when twenty-five cents was a fortune. There was a whole different set of values concerning money. This had such an impact on me that today it's still hard for me to purchase big-money items like a car, even when it is necessary."

SCOUTING OUT THE ENEMY

By the time America was recovering from the depression, a new challenge loomed. Nazi forces under an evil dictator named Hitler were engulfing much of Europe. And in the Pacific, fanatical soldiers, who were said to worship Emperor Hirohito, were overtaking much of Asia and had even attacked American forces at Pearl Harbor.

Both faith and patriotism motivated Holsinger. He enlisted in the Reserve Officers Corps, hoping to be able to finish his first semester of college and enter the Army Air Corps. But Uncle Sam needed ground troops in Europe and Asia, and Holsinger wound up in the infantry as a replacement in a veteran army unit. Due to his lack of seniority, he had no choice but to serve as a scout (or point man), one of the most dangerous assignments possible.

He landed on Guadalcanal Island in August 1943, where he and other members of the Twenty-fifth Infantry Division performed mop-up operations following nearly a year and a half of pitched battles with the Japanese forces.

Next, the division was shipped off for the invasion of Vella Lavella, a speck of land in the northern Solomon Islands group. Then after some rest and relaxation in New Zealand, Holsinger's contingent was dispatched to the island of New Caledonia for further training and preparation.

It was only when the soldiers were shipped off to the principal Philippine island of Luzon in the first weeks of 1945 that the fighting became unusually intense. Invaded by the Japanese in 1941, Luzon was the site of an embarrassing defeat for General Douglas MacArthur, who was forced to withdraw his troops to the Bataan Peninsula in December of that year. Months later, the troops were forced to surrender.

The U.S. Army returned to the Philippines for the initial landing on Leyte Island in the fall of 1944. Then it was on to Luzon on January 9, 1945, where they fought some 350,000 Japanese troops in what would become the largest land battle of the Pacific war.

Two days later, Holsinger landed on the island. As a scout, he led the way for his ten-man patrol, which went out ahead of larger squads and companies. On February 28, Holsinger would engage the enemy in a dangerous battle. His action would earn him the Silver Star.

Holsinger wrote about his experiences in the war and after in *Above the Cry of Battle,* a book he wrote with much difficulty and many tears. In the passage cited here, he recalls the events of that horrible day:

THE VIEW FROM THE FOXHOLE

Our patrol was moving out across no-man's-land toward Dig Dig, a strategic road junction. Jack and I were the two scouts for the day. We were seeking the enemy and checking out suspicious areas. We had been attacked the night before, so emotions and tensions were high, and we were certain that the enemy wasn't too far away.

Jack and I were moving slowly down a dusty road about 100 yards ahead of the rest of our unit. When we came to a small bridge, Jack went forward to check for booby traps. I was about 20 yards behind him with my rifle ready to cover him in case of enemy fire.

Suddenly, Jack went flat on his stomach. He had seen something suspicious, and waved me forward. Papers with Japanese printing littered the stream bed. Even worse, we could see a pair of feet in Japanese shoes!

I moved forward and joined Jack. He threw a grenade under the bridge, and we both jumped down off the bridge on either side. The grenade had finished off a Japanese soldier. "Now there's a good Japanese!" I said to myself before I reached down to check out the dead man's pockets. In the pocket closest to his heart, I found a photograph of a beautiful woman.

Some people might have felt sorry for the Japanese soldier, who would never be returning to the woman he loved. But to me, he was the enemy. And as with other enemy soldiers, all I could think about was how glad I was that he was dead.

It was on another day that Jack and I would make our way toward the Maringalo River. As the main body of troops rested, others searched up and down the river hoping to protect us from an ambush. The area was clear, and we crossed the river without incident.

On the right was a patch of high ground. Our captain chose this small, pear-shaped hill as the site where our company of 150 men would camp for the night. At about 4:30 that afternoon we started our foxholes. My six-man squad was told to dig our foxholes in a "V" shape surrounding the small part of the pear-shaped hill.

In front of us would be the enemy, but little did we know how close they were. In fact, an enemy observation point was hidden only by a small bush on a little knoll located only 130 meters away. Someone had been watching our every move.

I was on guard at about 1:30 A.M. the next morning. Everything seemed calm and peaceful. In order to keep myself awake I was reviewing the Sermon on the Mount. These three chapters of Matthew contained Jesus' words on forgiveness and so much more.

Suddenly I heard a scuffle, then frightening screams and shouts from a few yards away that pierced the night air. Three members of my squad had been attacked in their foxholes on one side of the "V." They didn't have time to raise their rifles. Instead, they used fists and anything else they could grab to defend themselves against enemy bayonets.

I heard thuds as my comrades' bodies were thrown out of their foxholes, which were quickly reoccupied by Japanese soldiers. I shot my rifle toward the enemy that now occupied my comrades' positions.

Next the Japanese used grenades to attack the three foxholes on my side of the "V." The attack left our sergeant injured, and he crawled back toward the main body of our troops. That left two of us.

A Japanese grenade rolled into the foxhole of Jake, my nearest companion. Before he could respond, the grenade exploded, covering me with smoke and dust. A brave soldier risked his life to drag Jake back to the main contingent.

Now it was just me, but did the Japanese know that? And would they rush at me?

I had been praying to God since that attack began. Now, my prayers became even more intense. I prayed that God would calm my pounding heart. While praying, I was given an idea. I shouted back to my comrades for mortar fire. I thought that if they could land shells in close to my foxhole, that would keep the enemy at bay.

Soon, I heard the telltale whistle of an incoming mortar shell. I hunkered down in my foxhole and waited for the explosion. The impact was so close that a cloud of dirt covered me, making it difficult to breathe. In a few seconds, another shell came in, then another, and another.

After each shell landed, I rose up slightly out of my foxhole, firing my rifle.

As the shelling and firing continued, I prayed another prayer to God: that He would enable me to hang on until daylight.

During the dark morning hours, a soldier joined me with a bag of grenades. As my ammunition was about to run out, I saw the first few streaks of light fill the night sky. And I could hear the few enemy soldiers trying to retreat with their wounded comrades.

Full daylight exposed the carnage that surrounded me. I had been squatting for hours, and it was only with difficulty that I could stand up straight once again. When I did, I saw dead and wounded comrades. One man who had survived in a nearby foxhole had his hand nearly severed when he reached out to stop a bayonet from piercing his chest.

On the floor of my own foxhole there were two fins from mortar shells. These reminded me how close death had come.

My captain congratulated me. "You single-handedly saved the company by holding your ground," he said.

But I knew the whole event was a miracle! God had spared my life.

AN INNER BATTLE

When it was time to hand out an award for bravery, the U.S. Army gave the award to Holsinger, not to God. The official citation for his Silver

Star reads in part: "Although he was alone, with no thought of retreat he coolly returned fire and directed assault mortar fire on the enemy not more than five yards from his position. He held his position for one hour until joined by another soldier carrying hand grenades. At dawn he assisted in clearing the enemy from the positions they had taken."

Holsinger had earned the respect of his comrades, and when the Japanese were at a safe distance, he felt comfortable. Still, anger and hatred for the enemy continued to gnaw at him.

Some people might say these feelings were justified. After all, he had nearly lost his life more than once, and he had witnessed many of his comrades go down around him.

Even more, his time on Luzon brought him face-to-face with some of the atrocities committed by Japanese soldiers. Some people have said that all is fair in love and war, but the enemy certainly seemed to take this approach to its ultimate conclusions.

It was routine for the enemy to booby-trap bodies—both American and Japanese alike. Many a U.S. soldier lost his life checking to see whether a comrade lying on the ground was dead or alive.

U.S. soldiers in jeeps also had to be constantly aware of running into a pianolike wire that the Japanese had strung across some of the Asian roads. More than one soldier was decapitated by this cruel weapon, causing army engineers to rig U.S. jeeps with protective hooks that would pull down such traps.

Even more disgusting were some of the atrocities routinely inflicted upon the innocent Filipino people whose country had become a battleground.

Filipino civilians often reported to U.S. command centers so they could receive food and medical examinations. One day, a Japanese soldier disguised himself as a Filipino civilian and approached a command center in the midst of a small group of Filipinos. When he got close enough to inflict harm, the soldier detonated the dynamite he wore on his body, instantly killing himself and causing death and terrible injury to many around him.

Filipinos who served as stretcher bearers for U.S. soldiers were often targets for Japanese soldiers, even though these Filipinos were unarmed and wore the white armband of the Red Cross.

Holsinger also remembers a Filipino woman telling a group of U.S. soldiers about the harrowing day when Japanese invaders occupied her village. She had been repeatedly raped by soldiers, her cries for help being ignored by nearby officers. Babies had been snatched from their mothers' arms and run through with bayonets. One soldier cut off the breast of a nursing mother. And a pregnant woman had been forced to strip naked and stand before her tormentors, who cut open her swollen stomach, leaving her to die unattended.

Thinking about such depravities only made Holsinger hate the Japanese even more. And while his anger may have helped fuel some of his battlefield heroics, it certainly didn't help his emotional life any.

"During the war and after, I had come to the conclusion that there was no reason to forgive the Japanese," he says. "Their treachery was too great, their evil too gross, the pain they inflicted too deep, the casualties too many, and the wounds too severe."

Although he isn't proud to say so, Holsinger admits that he felt a sense of glee when he stood over the body of a dead Japanese soldier. And he made a vow to avenge the death of every U.S. soldier by killing three or four enemy fighters. Clearly this was a man who subscribed to the wartime motto: "The only good Japanese is a dead one."

In time Holsinger concluded that this anger was sinful, but he justified it by telling himself that it was all part of fighting a "just" war.

In time Holsinger would release this hatred, but not before he returned home and began seeking God's will for the rest of his life.

RETURNING TO ASIA

After the Japanese surrendered in August 1945, Holsinger served as part of the occupation army in Japan. When he finally got home to Seattle later that year, he knelt down and kissed the ground.

As he did so, he said a simple prayer: "If it is all right with You, Lord, I never want to leave the States again."

Holsinger returned to Wheaton College where he finished the studies he had abandoned for the war. In 1949 he married Elisabeth (Betty) Hermansen, a fellow student, who was seated next to Holsinger on the first day of classes because his name came right after hers in the alphabetical listing.

After graduation Holsinger began work as an assistant football coach at Wheaton College, a job he could have enjoyed for many a year. But God had other plans.

When he had been a soldier in Asia, a frightened Holsinger had often turned to God for solace and comfort. Once, on the evening before his company expected to be involved in a particularly brutal battle, he went to a chapel tent and poured out his heart to God: "Lord, here is my life. I'll be and do whatever You want of me."

Now, as he was settling into a life of relative predictability and domesticity, he started praying again about God's will. At the time, thousands upon thousands of Christian veterans were returning to Asia to serve in some of the very places where they had once fought. In fact, so many World War II veterans responded to the call to serve overseas that they spawned a revival in missionary work whose effects can still be felt more than half a century later.

Holsinger considered going to Asia, but he wanted to do something different from what most missions organizations did. And as he thought about returning to Asia, he started having nightmares that brought back all the horrors of the war.

He continued to pray and seek counsel. He talked to his younger brother, Hap, who was already serving as a missionary to China, and to Dick Hillis, a veteran missionary in China.

Soon, Chuck and Betty were on their way to the Philippines with a Christian basketball team called Venture for Victory, which not only entertained U.S. troops but also shared the gospel. The ministry continues its work today, though it is now known as Sports Ambassadors.

Perhaps it's not surprising that Holsinger served God in such a way. After all, his two brothers and two sisters have been involved in ministry throughout their lives. The tradition continues today. All four of Chuck and Betty's children have been involved in Christian work overseas.

"There have been ministers in every generation of our family for three hundred years," says Holsinger with a mixture of humility and pride.

Changed from Within

Just about all the men and women who served in World War II say the conflict changed their lives. Holsinger is no different. "I would say that about 75 percent of the way I think and the way I look at challenges in life is because of the war," he says.

Even more important, the war changed the way thousands of Americans felt about overseas missionary service.

"One of the things I felt at the time was that God called some of us men into the military so that we would get a picture of the needs of the world," recalls Holsinger, who felt a strong desire to help bring healing to places overflowing with death and misery.

"I think one thing a lot of us asked ourselves after we had won the war was, What do we do now? Many of us felt it was a time for healing, a time to share the gospel.

"I don't think it was a guilt trip. Maybe it was for some people in some ways. But there was a burden that we felt. Because we had inflicted so

WHEATON'S POSTWAR
MISSIONARIES

Chuck Holsinger wasn t the only World War II veteran from Wheaton College who responded to the missionary call. In fact, historian and missionary David M. Howard says the war played a pivotal role in the postwar Golden Age of Missions.

The vision originally received by these men and women while overseas in the military and then stimulated and cultivated while at Wheaton College has borne fruit for half a century in missionary outreach, writes Howard in *From Wheaton to the Nations* (Wheaton College, 2001).

Among the cases Howard cites are the following:

¥ A group of soldiers serving in the occupation forces in the Philippines helped found Far Eastern Bible Institute and Seminary, the country s first interdenominational Bible training school.

¥ Members of the occupation force in Japan helped start the *GI Gospel Hour,* a Christian radio program. These veterans later founded the GI Gospel Crusade, which engaged in evangelistic outreach and community service for the Japanese people. (The organization was later renamed Far Eastern Gospel Crusade and continues its work today as SEND International.)

¥ Veterans who had worked with the *GI Gospel Hour* and similar efforts were instrumental in founding the

Interdenominational Foreign Missions Association, which helped coordinate the work of missions agencies throughout the world.

¥ And Dale Oxley, who as a marine had participated in the invasions of Saipan and Okinawa, returned to Japan as a missionary after completing his studies at Wheaton, even though he had received attractive offers to play football for two NFL teams. He and his wife served God in Japan for more than forty years.

According to historian David Howard, people like Oxley served as role models for later generations of missionaries: They set an example of visionary dedication and practical action, which continued throughout their lives and the lives of many whom they touched.

much carnage and damage on some of these countries, we felt that there had to be something else we could do to help the people recover.

"It was a feeling of being able to do something for the enemy. This in itself was an act of forgiveness in many ways."

Chuck Holsinger's book, *Above the Cry of Battle,* is available through bookstores nationwide.

Ready for battle. Private First Class Charles D. Holsinger (standing second from right) is shown with members of the squad he belonged to during the invasion of Luzon. To his right is scouting partner Lou Jandris, who was wounded during the first day of battle.

Finding fellowship. Holsinger (kneeling at lower right) spent time with these Christian friends, who were members of a regimental band.

Glad to be alive. For his action on the Philippine island of Luzon, Holsinger was given the Silver Star in June 1945.

TWELVE

GEORGE MASSOUD

ORTHODOX IN FAITH
AND PATRIOTISM

Shekry and Emma Massoud left their native country of Lebanon for the city of Danbury, Connecticut, in 1910. But once there, they didn't think of themselves as Lebanese-Americans. They were American-Americans through and through.

"Dad was very proud of being an American," says son George. "When my parents finally received their citizenship papers, they were as proud as peacocks."

George respected his parents' traditions, but his loyalty was to their new country, not their ancestral homeland. "I felt very, very loyal and very proud to be an American. It was the only country I ever knew."

Protestant and Catholic churches were plentiful in Danbury when Shekry and Emma arrived in the U.S. But their faith had been nourished in the Eastern Orthodox church of their native country. Finding no Orthodox churches in the west-side neighborhood where they lived, the Massouds went about starting one.

"They were among the founders of St. George Antiochian Orthodox

Church," says George, who remains an active member of the congregation to this day.

"I can still remember when we were children," explains George. "Some of the money my father earned as a hatmaker should have been going to our household and to food, but he was donating everything he could to build the church."

After the church opened in 1924, Shekry Massoud was there every Sunday, serving as a cantor and singing the beautiful Orthodox liturgies that have been sung around the world for centuries.

"He didn't have an operatic voice, but he was really dedicated," recalls George. "And he knew the prayers of the church inside and out. In fact, he would often correct the priests when they made mistakes."

From the day he was baptized, George was taught the principles of the faith at St. George's. The lessons he learned at church were reinforced at home: "There was an emphasis on honesty. That was a central value."

George also inherited a deep loyalty to America. That loyalty was so strong that he went down to the local navy recruiter's office on Friday, December 5, 1941, to enlist.

But his willingness to join the war effort worried his parents. "I had one heck of a job convincing my dad to sign off for me. And even if he hadn't, I would have gone anyway."

Other friends tried to talk him out of enlisting too. One was a veteran of World War I, who told George about the horrors of war. Another was a former navy man, who found out too late that he was unusually susceptible to seasickness. "He didn't last very long," says George. "The day he reported for duty he was discharged."

George listened to everything everyone said, but nothing could dim his enthusiasm. Then, two days after George visited the recruiter, Japanese airplanes attacked Pearl Harbor.

"I was saddened by the attack like everybody else," he says, "and real ticked off, to be honest with you."

America was now 100 percent behind the war effort. On Monday morning, the recruiter called George and told him to report for a physical exam. As soon as the doctors had given their OK, George was on his way to boot camp in Rhode Island.

Then two weeks later, he reported to the Brooklyn Naval Yards. George would be an apprentice seaman on the USS *Quincy*, a recently commissioned 13,600-ton heavy cruiser headed for the South Pacific.

To George, the ship seemed huge and invulnerable, but within months it would be one of twenty-four U.S. warships lost at Guadalcanal. That battle would test George's courage, his endurance, and his faith in God.

A NIGHT ILLUMINED BY FLAMES

By the middle of 1942, Japanese forces had taken control of dozens of Pacific islands. American commanders were particularly worried about Guadalcanal, which was located near the southeastern tip of the Solomon Islands group. Guadalcanal enjoyed a strategic location. That was why the Japanese had completed an airfield on the island in August, thus extending the reach of their air forces throughout the Pacific. U.S. forces were determined to reclaim Guadalcanal, which was the site of fierce land and naval battles.

The problems for Apprentice Seaman George Massoud and the hundreds of other crewmen of the *Quincy* began on Friday, August 7, the first day of the U.S naval campaign. The ship, which was patrolling the Surigao Strait, came under heavy attack from Japanese airplanes, whose bombs continued to fall on Saturday. Throughout the attacks, the *Quincy* avoided any direct hits, and U.S. Marines continued to land on Guadalcanal with relative ease.

Saturday evening, Massoud was on watch duty until midnight. He surveyed the seas all night for any signs of Japanese ships, but by the time his shift ended, all seemed clear. He fell into his bunk and a deep sleep.

That sleep was interrupted by the ship's alarms, which sounded around two in the morning. Japanese sailors, who had demonstrated their superiority in night-fighting techniques, started firing their guns and aiming their torpedoes at the *Quincy*.

"By the time I got to my battle station, all heck had broken loose," says Massoud. "The Japanese fleet had sneaked in on our entire group of destroyers and cruisers. All I could see and hear was the flashing and the booming of the guns on both sides, which seemed very close together."

The *Quincy* fired its big guns at the Japanese ships, but soon Massoud's ship had been caught in a fatal cross fire.

"It was the beginning of the end," he says. "We took quite a bit of shell fire and were hit with a couple of torpedoes. Our ship caught on fire."

From his position at the antiaircraft guns near the ship's bridge, Massoud witnessed a shell take out many of the ship's commanding officers. Massoud himself was wounded by shrapnel, for which he was later awarded the Purple Heart.

"I had a burning sensation in my arms and legs," he recalls.

Massoud doesn't remember there being a call to abandon the ship. He wasn't even sure that any commanders had been left alive to issue such a command.

"All I know is that when I got down to the main deck, the entire ship was listing very heavily to port. I decided it was about time to get off. Sometime between two-thirty and two-forty-five that morning, I jumped."

The sky was still dark, but the night was lit up by flames. "As I floated away from the ship, I could see that a number of our planes had taken direct hits and started to explode. As I looked back and saw her going down, there were a lot of fires illuminating everything. There was even fuel burning on the water, which created a smoky, rancid smell."

For the next four or five hours, Massoud bobbed on the turbulent waves and talked to God.

"I prayed all that Sunday morning while I was in the water," he says. "I remember repeating the Lord's Prayer over and over. I even promised God that I was going to be the nicest guy in the world if He would please get me out of this mess."

Alone and adrift, Massoud says he received comfort from an unusual source.

"I had lost my mom when I was a kid. She had always said she would be with me. I had a strange feeling that she was looking over me that night."

Massoud knew morning was approaching when streaks of light began to brighten the dark sky. Soon, he was rescued.

"The good Lord had to be on my side that night because we lost some four hundred men out of a crew of more than nine hundred."

In 1992, survivors erected a memorial honoring the men who died on the *Quincy*. A brief dedication on the memorial's plaque reads as follows:

> For those finest shipmates ever found,
> Who sailed the seas the world around,
> Now rest in peace at Savo Sound.

A PACIFIC DIARY

Massoud was fished out of the water and shipped off to a hospital on the island of New Caledonia for a month. There, doctors did all they could to remove the biggest pieces of shrapnel from his thighs and legs. They left the smaller pieces that had lodged closest to his bones. Then it was back to Danbury for thirty days of survivor's leave.

The American fleet had lost as many ships at Guadalcanal as the

Japanese had, but there was one major difference in the two countries' war efforts. America was building new destroyers at a rapid pace.

Soon Massoud was back at the Brooklyn Naval Yards with orders to board the USS *Monssen*.

"We waited until the ship was completed, put her in commission, and took her on a shakedown cruise to Bermuda and back. Then we proceeded to the South Pacific in early 1943."

For the next two and a half years, Massoud's naval record read like the diary of some of the major Pacific naval battles.

"Some days I can't remember my phone number," he says, "but I can still remember the name of all the islands I was on."

As the U.S. fleet approached the Mariana Islands, which are located some thirteen hundred miles southwest of Japan, Japanese fighter pilots staged an ill-fated attack. Historians now refer to the episode as "the Great Marianas Turkey Shoot."

At Saipan, one of the main Mariana Islands, American troops tried to capture another Japanese airfield and sought to sever Japanese communications lines. The *Monssen* provided fire support for marines who battled across the island in June and July.

From his perch on the ship, Massoud could see civilians who chose death over surrender, flinging themselves off the one-thousand-foot-tall "Suicide Cliff" on one end of the island. Days later, bodies of women and children could be seen floating in the sea around the ship.

"When you see something like that, you ask yourself, 'What the heck am I doing out here?' I didn't even know these people, but seeing them jump into the sea was disturbing.

"But you get over things like that quickly out there. You go on to the next battle or the next operation. You put it behind you, in part because you realize that either they're going to get you or you're going to get them."

Another Japanese airfield was located on Peleliu, a small, coral-fringed island that was part of the Palau island group. The *Monssen* and other ships bombarded the island for days, attempting to destroy hundreds of coral caverns that protected enemy soldiers. In the end, though, the island had to be taken through a monthlong marine combat campaign during the fall of 1944.

Iwo Jima was the next island to be bombarded. Its airfields were surrounded by hundreds of pillboxes and miles of tunnels and trenches.

ON TO OKINAWA

In April Americans attacked Okinawa, a mountainous island located midway between Japan and Formosa (now known as Taiwan). It was thought that building a U.S. airfield there would make it easier to reach mainland Japan. Knowing the strategic importance of the island, the Japanese dug in, killing more than twelve thousand U.S. servicemen—the highest death toll in any Pacific campaign.

The crew of the *Monssen* could tell the fighting for Okinawa was particularly intense. Massoud says that was the first time he and his fellow sailors encountered Japan's dreaded kamikaze pilots, who intentionally flew their planes into U.S. ships. During 1944 and 1945, the attacks had sunk or severely damaged at least six major ships.

The pilots' single-minded devotion to their cause inspired fear among the sailors, and seeing them heading toward his ship once again led Massoud to cry out to God.

"Either you hit them or they hit you," says Massoud, who manned the all-important antiaircraft guns. "I just opened fire and prayed that I would get them."

October took the *Monssen* to the Philippine island of Leyte and the largest naval battle in world history. Among the more than two hundred U.S. ships involved in the battle for Leyte Gulf were many battleships that had been repaired after being damaged at Pearl Harbor. Massoud was thrilled by the show of force, which resulted in a decisive U.S. victory and spelled the end of the Japanese navy.

"After the sinking of the *Quincy,* I had sort of a bitter feeling," he says. "But to see some of our old battleships like the *New York,* which were banged up in Pearl Harbor, brought back into duty gave me the biggest satisfaction. It felt like it was payback time."

Next, the *Monssen's* final assignment was delivering troops for the invasion of the Philippines. Then it was off to Alaska for some much-needed rest and relaxation. While Massoud and his crewmates were on shore, they heard their ship's whistles making a loud commotion. "I think the war is over," said the sailors. By October, Massoud was back in Danbury.

THE LIFE OF A HOMETOWN HERO

War changed George Massoud's life. For one thing, he returned to a hero's welcome. "I got to be well known in the community," he says. "I was one of the first local guys to be wounded. My story made the papers. Nearly everyone I ran into had heard about my experiences at Guadalcanal."

Massoud opened up a service station, George's Gulf, on the corner of Elm and New Streets. For the next twelve years, he talked to customers who came in for gas or an oil change.

His wartime exploits also put his maturation from a boy to a man on the fast track. "It made a man out of me very, very quickly," he asserts. "I gained a lot of self-confidence. I wouldn't say I became cocky, but I learned to stand up for my rights. If I felt I had something to say on a subject or could make a good argument, I did my best to put my point across."

This newfound confidence let to Massoud's entrance into local politics. "I had met so many people at the station. People felt that I was a pretty popular guy. When some friends asked me if I would be willing to take a shot at running for the city council on the Democratic ticket, I decided to give it a try."

Massoud served as a councilman during the 1970s, then won election as the city clerk. His unsuccessful bid to become Danbury's mayor in 1978 ended his political career, but nothing could stop Massoud from being involved in his community.

He's also involved with fellow veterans who gather every morning to share war stories.

"A lot of my service seems like a very distant memory," he says, "but when I sit down with our group of army men, marines, and sailors over cups of coffee, we talk about the old days, and the war stories really flow."

He used to attend reunions of sailors who served on the *Quincy* and the *Monssen,* but lately World War II veterans have been dying off, to be replaced by veterans of the Korean conflict. "I feel lost not being with the people I served with."

SERVING AT ST. GEORGE'S

There was one other important thing that changed for Massoud after the war. Soon after he got back, he married Mary Attick in a ceremony at St. George Antiochian Orthodox Church.

He even served on the church's board of trustees. During his tenure, the congregation decided to build a new church to replace the original building that had been funded with so much love by his father.

He's not on the board anymore. "I thought it would be good to step back and let the younger generation come in," he says. Part of that younger generation is his own son Mark, who serves on the board of trustees now. Mark's daughter Gabrielle is a star pupil in the church's second-grade Sunday school class.

George is proud to see members of the Massoud family rooted in the church. Such connections represent the old Middle Eastern traditions of this now thoroughly American family.

A welcome recruit. George Massoud had enlisted in the U.S. Navy on December 5, 1941. After the attack on Pearl Harbor two days later, he was quickly sent to the South Pacific aboard the USS Quincy.

A rest before tragedy. On leave from training camp, Apprentice Seaman George Massoud hugs his sister as a friend looks on. Massoud would soon be fighting for his life.

A sacred place. George Massoud and Mary Attick are married at St. George Antiochian Orthodox Church, which his parents helped build.

THIRTEEN

JOE AND KITTY SULLIVAN

A WARTIME MEMORY ALBUM

If a picture is worth a thousand words, the memory album assembled by the family of the late Joseph Sullivan is a major opus.

As his daughter Judy wrote, "These are excerpts from the lives of two sweethearts during the most turbulent times of the twentieth century.

"These two young people from the streets of Philadelphia were caught up in the turmoil of a war that would change not only their lives but the very core of a young and innocent country."

The memory album could fill an entire book. On the following pages are just a few of the highlights.

A WEDDING LONG DELAYED

Although they were two teenagers growing up in Philadelphia, Joe Sullivan and Kitty (Katherine) McNally didn't meet at school. He attended West Catholic Boys High School, and she attended West Catholic Girls High School.

Instead, the two met through mutual friends who frequented a local delicatessen. They became better acquainted at neighborhood dances. When one of Kitty's girlfriends said, "Joe likes you," Kitty knew it was true.

The two were engaged in 1941, and they were at Kitty's home listening to the radio when a news bulletin interrupted the music. Pearl Harbor had been attacked. The announcement also interrupted their marriage plans. Joe enlisted in the Army Air Corps in March 1942 and left for training.

Their courtship continued through letters, with Joe telling Kitty, "When I graduate and I get my commission, then I'll have something to offer you."

Joe did get his commission and his Air Corps wings. Kitty traveled across the country by train so the two could be married on November 13, 1943, in the chapel at the Walla Walla, Washington, Army Air Base. The next month, Joe shipped out to Europe.

"We were in love," says Kitty. "I had a lot of faith in him coming home, and I wanted to have a baby."

BRAVERY IN THE SKY

Second Lieutenant Joseph M. Sullivan was the bombardier for the ten-man crew on the *Little Colonel*, a B-17 Flying Fortress based in England.

Kitty liked how he looked in his leather flight jacket. She was even more proud when she read about his exploits in the *Philadelphia Inquirer*.

"Phila. Air Marksman Routs 4 Nazi Planes," said the headline. The article described how Sullivan had shot down one of the attacking enemy planes.

"I started to track him into range at about 900 yards," he said. "I knew I had to get him so I fired about 150 rounds at him.

"As he spiraled down through the clouds, the co-pilot yelled, 'You got him!,' and it sure made me feel good."

Then the crew of the *Little Colonel* continued the flight to a German war plant where they successfully completed their bombing mission and returned safely to England.

"I Knew Something Was Wrong"

Joe and Kitty wrote each other regularly, so when his letters stopped coming, she feared the worst.

"He was great at writing," she says. "So when I hadn't had a letter in many weeks, I knew something was wrong."

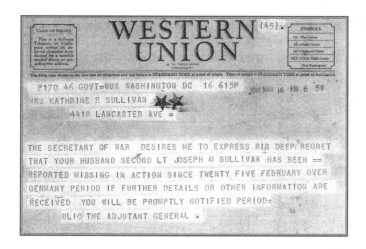

On March 8, 1944, Kitty learned she was pregnant.

The following week, she was in the third-floor apartment she shared with her mother when the doorbell rang.

Running down the stairs, she met a Western Union man on his way up. "He handed me the telegram like it was a birthday greeting," she recalls.

She opened the telegram on the stairs. She immediately saw a telltale symbol—two five-pointed stars—and knew it was bad news.

In May a Brooklyn woman whose husband was a prisoner of war was listening to a shortwave radio broadcast from Berlin. In the broadcast she heard that Joe was a prisoner, too, and was uninjured and in good health. The woman was one of many who wrote to Kitty and shared similar information. "Hope this will mean good news for you," she wrote.

"THE LAST MISSION"

In prison Joe used words and a drawing to document the last mission of the *Little Colonel* on February 25, 1944.

"Visibility was poor, and the coast of northern France greeted us with scattered bursts of ugly black clouds from flak guns," he wrote.

"The navigator called out some of the historic places we were flying over. He said it looked as if it was going to be a sightseeing trip. We sincerely hoped he was right."

But he wasn't. Enemy planes were attacking the Allied squadron.

"We tried to drop back from the rest of the group, and then we were cold meat. We were riddled from nose to tail twice by attack from directly overhead."

The plane was badly damaged and was rapidly losing altitude. The entire crew bailed out, some barely missing being hit by the pilotless plane. Joe landed in the square of a rural village and was immediately surrounded by hostile townspeople brandishing pitchforks and clubs.

Curiously Joe's description of the episode omits his own act of bravery. Before parachuting off the plane, he checked to make sure everyone else had safely bailed out.

That was when he saw Paul Teetor, the plane's navigator. Paul was hanging out of the bomb bay door, his legs entangled in massive cables that dangled from the damaged door.

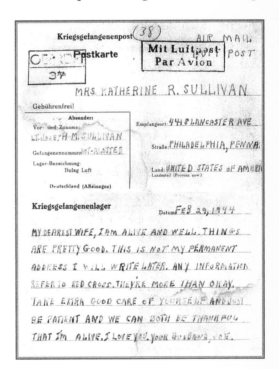

With the burning plane plummeting toward the ground, Joe wrestled with the cables until Paul was freed. Later, when Paul saw Joe in a prison camp, he was surprised that his rescuer had made it off the plane before it crashed.

After the war, Joe was awarded the Silver Star for his bravery and heroism.

"I Am Alive and Well"

Four days after his plane had been shot out of the sky, Joe wrote Kitty a brief but affectionate postcard. "Things are pretty good," he said. Kitty would not receive the postcard for months.

"Thank God, You're Alive"

It would be June before Joe was moved to the Stalag Luft 1 prisoner-of-war camp. For the past four months, he had been at a series of transit camps.

When Kitty finally had an address where she could write him, she poured out her feelings in a letter that filled nearly every millimeter of the government-issued form.

It was also her first chance to tell Joe that she was expecting a baby in the fall.

Prayers for the Impossible

Throughout Joe's imprisonment, Kitty prayed to God for his safe return.

"I prayed to St. Jude, the patron saint of desperate situations and hopeless cases. When I prayed, I said, 'If you bring Joe back, I will name the baby in your honor.'"

Judy was born on September 16, which was also Kitty's birthday.

"When I told the nurse it was my birthday, she said, 'I think you're going to get a present,'" remembers Kitty.

Joe heard about the birth in November, and told Kitty how he felt in a letter.

"The same birthday for two wonderful girls," he wrote. "I only wish I had ten pages to fill with all I have to say. I'll just have to put it off till I get home and show and tell you at the same time."

LIFE IN CAMP

Joe was a prisoner of war for fifteen months. The YMCA prepared "War Time Log" books that were distributed by the Red Cross to Allied prisoners along with food and supplies. Joe filled his log book with written ramblings and drawings of prison life.

The drawing of Joe sitting at a table in a prison bunkhouse looks almost homey. So does Joe's description of Christmas 1944.

"Christmas Eve brought five different types of cookies and hot chocolate," he wrote.

"Thanks to the Red Cross we had about as enjoyable a Christmas as could be possible under the circumstances. The whole room worked together and cooked and baked for three days in preparation for it."

But Joe's drawing of the guard tower clearly shows that camp life was no picnic.

"WE HAVE A DATE TONIGHT"

Joe's camp was liberated by the Russians in May 1945, but he didn't get home until July.

"Joe looked good, but he was a lot more quiet than he usually was," says Kitty. "I could tell from his pensiveness that he had been through hell."

But their love was still alive.

In 1946 Joe and Kitty had another daughter, the second of four children. Joe rejoined the air force after giving civilian life a brief try. After the Korean War broke out, he was called up for active service, and his bomber group was part of the first U.S. deployment to Korea.

During the 1962 Cuban Missile Crisis, Joe was in an armed B-47 that was ready to go at a moment's notice.

In time, says Kitty, "I became a more seasoned air force wife."

Joe retired in 1972 as a lieutenant colonel. He died in 1983.

"At times it was scary, sad, and lonely," says Kitty, "but it was a good life."

FOURTEEN

JIM DOWNING

NAVIGATING SOULS
TOWARD HEAVEN

The practical necessities of making ends meet during Depression-era America—not a sudden outpouring of patriotic fervor—led Jim Downing to walk into the navy recruiter's office in Hannibal, Missouri, on September 22, 1932.

"It was the height of the economic depression," says Downing, who remembers how hard it was for his banker father to support a wife, a sister, and three sons on ninety dollars a month. "My idea was to save money, get out of the service, go to college and law school, and then get into politics."

He signed on for a four-year stint, but he didn't think he would ever face combat. In 1936, when he extended his enlistment for two more years, there were hints that America might someday go to war.

"President Roosevelt started a ship-building program, and we were building up the navy," he recalls. "And we were aware that there were dangers from the other side of both oceans."

The signs of war's approach were increasing by the summer of 1941. "America had cut off oil exports to Japan, we had temporarily detained some of their ships, and Roosevelt had said the U.S. would not allow increased occupations of China," says Downing.

Japan sought to calm American nerves by sending an ambassador, who promised peace. "I saw the ambassador's seaplane land in Hawaii on Friday, two days before the Pearl Harbor attack, and I saw it take off on Saturday for Washington," remembers Downing.

Navy men like Downing were so optimistic about America's fighting strength that even if a conflict were forthcoming, they assumed the best. Their optimism was fueled by propaganda that poured forth from official channels.

"Perhaps we could confront the Japanese, but the battle would last months, not years. Plus, we thought they couldn't shoot straight. And as for the battle for naval superiority, we had been led to believe that everything stamped with the phrase 'Made in Japan' was cheap. Surely they would be no match for American might."

Of course, things didn't turn out so rosy, as Downing and the rest of America discovered on December 7, 1941. His ship, the USS *West Virginia*, was one of many ships damaged or sunk at Pearl Harbor.

Downing wasn't on the ship when it was hit by six eighteen-inch aircraft torpedoes in the port side and two fifteen-inch armor-piercing bombs. But he was back at Pearl Harbor in twenty minutes after the attack, caring for the wounded and helping put out the raging fires.

The bombs had wreaked havoc on the ship's superstructure deck, and the torpedoes had caused extensive flooding. But unlike the USS *Oklahoma*, which was moored nearby, the *Wee Vee* didn't sink.

A quick-thinking damage control officer ordered the flooding of some of the ship's starboard-side compartments, and the vessel rested upright in forty feet of water, its keel settling snugly on the harbor bottom. Half a year later, when the ship's hull was patched and it was pumped out and refloated for repairs, the bodies of seventy dead sailors were found in the lower holds.

Once war had begun, there was no way for sailors to get out of the navy, even if they wanted to. And by that time, Downing's perspective on life had radically changed. He no longer dreamed of a life in politics. Rather, he went on to serve as the commanding officer of a ship in the Korean War, retiring in 1956 after a twenty-four-year naval career.

But ultimately it wasn't the love of country or battle that kept him in the service. It was the love of God. Downing firmly believed that the military provided him with the perfect opportunity to minister to the men and women serving their nation.

"I tried to find God's will in making major decisions," says Downing, "and it was clear that the navy was the place for me to invest my life.

"As I saw it, I was going to do this as long as God wanted me here. I was going to be in the navy until He wanted me out."

THE DAWN OF THE NAVIGATORS

Jim Downing was born on August 22, 1913, in bustling Kansas City, Missouri, but grew up in tiny Plevna, Missouri, which was founded by Bulgarian immigrants. (He keeps a map handy to point out the town to those who have never heard of it, which is most folks.)

The most prominent institutions in the town were its three churches. But whether the denomination was Disciples of Christ, Methodist, or Southern Baptist, Downing says they all promoted a watered-down version of American civil religion that did little to touch the soul.

"In our small town, church was the center of social life. And as children reached junior-high age, they were expected to go forward, make a decision to become a Christian, and be baptized.

"But it didn't mean much to many of us. It was just part of our cultural life and didn't have much of an impact on how people lived. As we jokingly said, it was more like this: 'Meet Christ at the altar and tell Him you'll see Him in heaven, with nothing expected in between.'"

Downing outgrew this lukewarm gospel soon after he was in the service.

"Somewhere along the way, I had heard a slogan that went, 'I've lived today.' I thought that was what I would do in the navy—seize the day and live life to its fullest. But even though I learned a lot and got to travel a lot, I never found the type of living the slogan described."

Downing would soon be exposed to a more vibrant brand of Christianity that seemed tailor-made for a sailor like him. That exposure came through an organization called the Navigators, an international organization that introduces the unchurched to the faith and encourages Christians to achieve spiritual maturity.

The ministry's motto is simple and direct: "To know Christ and make Him known." After his retirement from the navy, Downing worked as an executive with the organization for three decades. He is still affiliated with it as he nears ninety.

The Navigators had its beginnings with Servicemen's Bible Studies Clubs, which were hosted by an energetic southern Californian named Dawson Trotman.

Those who knew Trotman in the 1920s didn't consider him the type to have much to do with religion. A habitual ne'er-do-well who frequently wound up in jail, he ended up behind bars once again in 1926. That time proved to be different, though, as he realized he had hit life's bottom and prayed a desperate prayer for redemption.

Two days later, he walked right past a familiar pool hall and attended a church meeting instead. There he agreed to memorize a few Bible verses. Three weeks later, as he headed for his job at a lumberyard, the verses came alive in his heart. Soon, he asked Christ to forgive his sins, and he dedicated his life to serving God.

Trotman immediately began to share his newfound faith with coworkers at the lumberyard, strangers he met on the street, and just about anyone else he encountered. His evangelistic efforts weren't an accident, but the intentional result of a solemn pledge. Trotman had promised God he would share his faith with at least one person every day.

There's even a story in Navigator circles that demonstrates his dedication to this goal. According to the story, Trotman was lying in bed one night when he realized he hadn't spoken to anyone about Christ that day. He jumped out of bed, hurriedly dressed himself, and hit the streets looking for a hungry soul.

In 1933 Trotman met Les Spencer, a navy man assigned to the USS *West Virginia*, which was docked at San Pedro, north of Los Angeles.

Trotman never served in the military. ("He never could have passed the physical," muses Downing.) But under Trotman's tutelage, Spencer began telling other navy men about Jesus. Those men, in turn, told others, just as they had been trained.

Jim Downing was the sixth man to become a Christian through these efforts.

"I remember a sailor who was hard at work early one morning," states Downing. "He was singing, and he had a shining face. I concluded that he had an inner resource that wasn't affected by outward circumstances. I wanted the quality of life he had, so they took me over to meet Dawson Trotman."

In 1935 a twenty-two-year-old Downing invited Jesus to take charge of his life. He was far from the last convert reached by such means. By 1943 more than one thousand navy ships and other military addresses included at least one Navigator on board. After the war the ministry spread throughout the U.S. By the end of 2001, the ministry had an annual income of more than $100 million and worked in 107 countries.

A Peace That Passes Understanding

World War II changed Jim Downing's life in many ways.

The morning of the attack on Pearl Harbor, he and Morena, his wife of six months, were with others at the home of a local Navigator couple. As he ate breakfast, he thought about a class he would be teaching two hours later at the Honolulu Bible Training School. His thoughts were interrupted shortly before 8:00 A.M. by gunfire and explosions. Then a local radio station announced the attack.

Downing and other sailors hopped in a car and began the six-mile journey toward the harbor. They were unable to see the damage, which was hidden from their view by mountains, but as they reached the end of the Kalihi Valley, the entire tragic scene opened up before them.

"My first reaction was one of anger," he says. "I was disappointed in America's political and military leadership. Anytime you have military leaders who have no combat experience, they're vulnerable to surprise attacks like this because they think it can't happen.

"Right then, I vowed that if I ever was in a position of authority, something like this would never happen to us again."

Downing also experienced powerful surges of patriotism: "I was proud of our efforts to get in there and win the war."

In time, though, the realities of the conflict settled in, and the next feeling that came over him was resentment.

"I highly resented having four years taken out of my life," he says. "I felt as if Japan and Germany were dictating the conditions of my life during that period. I wasn't free to make any choices."

Especially galling was Downing's forced separation from Morena. She and other U.S. civilians were evacuated from Hawaii and returned to the mainland. The two newlyweds would not see each other for a year and a half.

But the pressures of wartime also brought about at least one positive effect. The superheated atmosphere of war helped refine Downing's faith, continuing the spiritual transformation that had begun years ago.

"The greatest permanent difference the war made in my life was that

I discovered a sense of deep, inner peace that remains even when I get shook up about something," he says.

Demonstrating his Navigator training, which emphasizes memorizing Scripture, Downing quotes two verses from Paul's epistle to the Philippians: "Do not be anxious about anything, but in everything, by prayer and petition, with thanksgiving, present your requests to God. And the peace of God, which transcends all understanding, will guard your hearts and minds in Christ Jesus" (4:6–7).

Downing doesn't believe that being a Christian means that life will be a bowl of cherries. Instead, he has seen that God provides a comfort that provides hope and calming in the midst of chaos. He explains, "It isn't like God is saying, 'I'm going to deliver you from death,' but rather a sense of divine peace that says everything's OK and that even if it's your time to go, you're ready."

Downing recalls one time when the ship he was on collided with a French-owned vessel.

"I had this sense of divine peace, even though I was convinced everything was going to blow up," he says. Thankfully the crash did not result in damaged fuel tanks or a blazing inferno.

"But frankly I was a little bit let down that I didn't die then," he says. "I wasn't anxious to leave my wife, but I had thought my next sight would be in heaven. Instead, I was on the bridge dealing with a big hole in the ship."

Downing finds that this divine peace continues to be a powerful presence in his life: "Even today when I get shook up about something, I know there is no real threat and the fear is a false alarm. If there were real danger, God would supply that deep peace."

TEACHING BY WORD AND EXAMPLE

Downing remained with the *West Virginia* as it was being repaired and fitted for battle in the Pacific. In the evenings and on the weekends, he

THE NAVIGATORS AND WORLD MISSIONS

As one of the pioneering members of the Navigators, navy veteran Jim Downing has had a front-row seat to the growth of one of the twentieth century s major Christian organizations.

Here are some of his observations, taken from a paper he wrote:

During the 39 years between 1950 and 1989 the population of the world doubled. During the same period the number of people on earth who call themselves Christians more than doubled increasing from 854,000,000 to 1,722,000,000.

After the end of World War II, the number of Christian missionaries serving overseas started increasing and grew rapidly from about 18,000 to more than 150,000 today.

According to many experts, this burst of Christian outreach grew out of men impacted by God while serving in the military before and during World War II. Among the groups involved in fueling this movement was the Navigators.

Navigators founder Dawson Trotman codified a number of approaches to Christian growth, Bible reading, prayer, and evangelism.

One of these approaches became known as the NAVIGATOR WHEEL, which portrayed Christ as the center of life. From this hub radiated spokes on the wheel, such as studying the Word of God, praying, living a radiant Christian life, having an outreach in evangelism, and helping Christians grow spiritually.

Beginning in 1933, the U.S. Navy served as the laboratory where Trotman s disciples applied this teaching tool. Sailors had a daily break in their schedules between 6:00 and 7:30 P.M. That 90 minutes was prime time for evangelism which we took advantage of daily.

One of the strengths of the Battleship laboratory was that every new Christian had a role model. When a sailor made the decision to follow Christ he knew exactly what he was expected to do and learned how to do it from his spiritual father.

Navy men who re-enlisted for an additional term could choose the ship where they would serve their next assignments. Navigators leaders routinely prayed over a list of ships to determine where we wanted to send one of our team members. In addition, Christian sailors brought their non-Christian friends to Navigator homes, where they heard the Gospel.

At the conclusion of World War II, Trotman encouraged those who had been impacted by the Navigator ministry to go overseas as missionaries. Soon Navigators were accepted by and serving with more than forty Mission Agencies.

Trotman also conducted a speaking tour at Bible schools and Christian colleges. Some 400 students said they had enrolled in these schools after coming out of the Navigators military ministry.

One missionary executive said, It is hard to find a mission leader today whose life has not been significantly impacted by the Navigators.

When God called Dawson Trotman to minister to a few sailors, little did he realize how God would use military men and women to further missionary work around the world.

led Bible studies for fellow sailors, earning the affectionate nickname "Deacon."

"I stayed at Pearl Harbor with the ship until she was raised in 1943, and that was the most profitable time of my life," he says. "There were hundreds of guys on base who had nothing to do after dark, so we would gather in air raid shelters and study the Bible. It was a real profitable time."

Once the *West Virginia* returned to sea, Downing returned to America where he was reassigned to training and supervisory duties.

During the Korean War, he was the commanding officer of the USS *Patapsco,* a seaplane support ship that provided fuel and communications support for combat aircraft. Downing wanted his 125 men to like him, but he discovered that there are some people in every crowd who resent authority and do everything they can to rebel against it.

"They resented me because I symbolized authority, so I had to run a tighter ship," he says.

There were other men, though, who appreciated Downing's principled leadership. Many of the men attended the Sunday morning Divine Services where he taught the Bible.

After war's end, Downing returned to Washington, D.C., where he served as an instructor at the navy's New Construction Gunners' Mate School.

Just as he had always done, he spent weekends teaching the Bible. He helped organize a program called the Central Union Mission Servicemen's Center. Meanwhile, Morena threw herself into women's ministry, helping start the Servicewomen's Christian Fellowship.

One of the lessons Downing taught at the center was based on Paul's message in 2 Corinthians 1:10: "He has delivered us from such a deadly peril, and he will deliver us." In the lesson, Downing described deliverance as an ongoing process, not a once-and-for-all event. "I taught that salvation represents deliverance from the penalty of sin, from the power of sin, and ultimately from the presence of sin," he says.

STILL TEACHING

Today, Downing is a spry eighty-nine.

"I have come to see that the secret of long life is to choose good grandparents," says Downing. He ought to know. A great-grandfather lived to be ninety-four, and both a sister and a brother are now over ninety.

And, of course, Downing is still teaching the Bible any chance he gets.

He remains active in Navigator activities, conducts several weekly Bible studies, volunteers his time as a lay counselor, serves as a consultant to the U.S. Center for World Mission in Pasadena, California, and helps other ministries. He also speaks at conferences around the world.

Ever since the September 11, 2001, attacks on the World Trade Center and the Pentagon, military chaplains have been inviting him to talk to green soldiers who are preparing for their first battle and may want to know a little about the divine peace that has comforted Downing for more than sixty-five years.

He also continues to act as a "Deacon" to the men who served on the *Wee Vee,* but now as the chaplain for the USS *West Virginia* Reunion Association.

"I still keep in contact with some of the people I witnessed to sixty to seventy years ago," he says, "and it's remarkable how many of them have become Christians over the years."

At the association's May 2001 reunion in Minneapolis, Downing presided over a Divine Service at which he spoke about the resurrected Christ. His text for his message was found in the words of Jesus quoted in John 11:25–26: "I am the resurrection and the life. He who believes in me will live, even though he dies; and whoever lives and believes in me will never die."

After the message, some of the *West Virginia* veterans approached Downing, asking, "Do you remember the time you talked to me about the Bible and Jesus back on the ship?"

Invariably Downing remembers.

Some of Jim Downing's stories about life in the navy can be found in the "Stories" section of the USS *West Virginia* Association's Web site (http://www.usswestvirginia.org). Downing is also the author of a book titled *Meditation.* Copies are available from Dawson Media (call 719-594-2100, or go to www.dawsonmedia.com).

Picture perfect. The Wee Vee *in better days.*

Ready to serve. Jim Downing walked into the navy recruiter's office on September 22, 1932. Nine years later he was a navy man stationed on the USS West Virginia.

Pounded at Pearl Harbor. The USS West Virginia *was hit by torpedoes and bombs on December 7, 1941, coming to rest on the harbor bottom. When the ship was refloated for repairs, the bodies of 70 dead sailors were found in the lower holds.*

FIFTEEN

RICHARD KIM

FIGHTING FOR WHAT'S RIGHT

In a sense everyone's life can be seen as a journey. But Richard Kim's life journey has certainly had more geographical twists and spiritual turns than most of us have experienced.

He was born in Korea, but his family moved to China before he was a year old to escape political oppression. While still in his teens, Kim joined U.S. forces in Asia. He moved to America and assumed that his military career would end after World War II. But he served in Korea and Vietnam before retiring from the military and becoming an Episcopal priest.

"I laid down the crossed rifles of an airborne infantry officer in the Green Berets to pick up the cross of Jesus," he says.

Kim still serves as a spiritual leader, but he's no longer in the Episcopal Church. Just as social upheavals of the 1960s and 1970s changed the way some Americans viewed the military, the spiritual upheavals that erupted during the same time shook the foundations of many churches and denominations.

Both his political views and his Christian theology have been challenged over the past few decades. But as Kim sees it, the eternal verities are unchanging, and it is for these he will continue to fight, no matter where his journey takes him.

WARS AND RUMORS OF WARS

Americans entered World War II in 1941, but by that time, people in China had been fending off Japanese aggression for a decade.

Richard Kim knew nothing of these problems when he was born in Seoul, Korea, in 1927. Nevertheless, international political conflicts were already having an impact on his young life.

Kim's father, Dr. Chang Sei Kim, was a U.S.-trained, freedom-loving medical doctor in Korea, which had been under Japanese control since the late 1800s. Dr. Kim, along with his brother-in-law, Dosan Ahn Chang Ho, was involved in founding the Korean Independence Movement, which brought both men to the attention of the Japanese authorities. (Dr. Kim died in New York in 1934, but in 2000 he was recognized posthumously by the Korean government as one of the founders of modern Korea.)

In 1928 the family hastily moved to Shanghai, China. Within a few years, Japanese armed forces were making incursions into China, and by 1937 the two countries were at war. To make matters worse, China was facing severe internal divisions, as Nationalists and Communists battled each other for supremacy.

Growing up in a cosmopolitan city like Shanghai during those troubled and uncertain times gave young Richard Kim an unusually multicultural background.

"By birth I was a Korean, but regarded myself as a Chinese, and of course American, even in infancy," he says.

His affection for America came from his family, from American friends, children of U.S. business and missionary families, and fellow students at the Shanghai American School. That's where he and his friends were when they first heard about the attack at Pearl Harbor. "I can recall the morning distinctly," he says.

By early 1942, Japanese soldiers in China began rounding up people thought to be potential troublemakers. For the Kim family, political upheaval had once again made their home city unsafe.

"The Japanese began to round up all heads of families for internment," says Kim. In time Kim's brother Peter was arrested and imprisoned by the Japanese secret police. Peter, who had extensive contacts with American business interests in China, was suspected of being an American spy. Although he was eventually released, he underwent intense torture and interrogation.

"Prior to his arrest, we had been making plans to escape from Shanghai. By this time I was sixteen. The Japanese were oppressing people of my age, forcing them to take Japanese language lessons and generally trying to recruit or cultivate a younger group.

"My family would have nothing to do with that, so we chose to escape."

ESCAPE FROM SHANGHAI

In May 1944, Kim and more than a dozen other Shanghai residents began their monthlong trek west toward Free China. They boarded a train to Hangchow, a resort community southwest of Shanghai, where they got on a boat that took them down the Yangtze River. From there, members of the group traveled by trucks and junks (small boats) in their quest to reach Free China—which was as yet free from Japanese control.

"Because of the fighting, we had to alter our travel plans several times," he says. "And as we went westward, the Japanese army kept thrusting westward, making our efforts to reach Free China more difficult."

As he journeyed westward, heading to an uncertain destination, Kim was shored up by the one unchanging thing he knew he could rely on—his faith in God.

"My family had always gone to a Presbyterian-type community church in Shanghai," he says. "That's where I went every Sunday as I was growing up. But it had never meant that much to me.

"When I was sixteen, and preparing for our escape, I accepted Jesus Christ as my Savior and Lord. I knew I would never survive this whole thing without that faith. Among my belongings, I concealed a little Bible, which was a bit risky considering it was in English and we were traveling as Chinese 'refugees.'

"It was when our group left Shanghai that Jesus became very personal to me. We were leaving home, and I was leaving my mother, two brothers, and a sister behind. It was just me, an older brother, and our group going into the unknown.

"At this point, Jesus became a friend and sustainer. There were many times when traveling was dangerous, confronting not only combatants, but roving bandits. There were times when we just didn't know what would happen. Yet because of my faith, I knew." By the end of 1944, U.S. forces were trying to recruit Asians who know local languages and customs. Thus a seventeen-year-old Kim enlisted in the U.S. Army in the deep interior of Free China.

"America was at war, fighting against the Japanese and the Germans," he says. "Even though my brother had arranged for me to fly the Hump [Himalayan Mountains] to India, and ultimately New York to attend school, I felt keenly that I wanted to volunteer to fight. I felt a duty to enlist. So I enlisted in the army by lying about my age."

Staff Sergeant Kim served out the last few months of the war as a clerk in the Allied headquarters in China. After the atomic bombs were dropped on Japan and surrender seemed imminent, he was part of the first contingent of Allied forces to enter Shanghai.

In the fall of 1946 he was discharged from the army in California, and went on to Mount Hermon School in Massachusetts to finish up his high-school education.

"I loved everything about America. I loved singing 'God bless America' and the national anthem. I loved everything she stood for."

But things haven't always turned out as expected in Kim's life, and within a few years he was on his way back to Asia once again.

KOREA CALLING

After World War II, Kim studied at Dickinson College in Carlisle, Pennsylvania, on the GI Bill. He also enlisted in the Pennsylvania National Guard, but he didn't think that would lead him back into combat.

"I had thought that once I had left the military, I would be out once and for all because I really didn't want any part of it anymore," he says.

"But lo and behold, the situation in Korea erupted, and the country was talking about federalizing some of the state National Guard divisions. As it turned out, one of the four divisions President Truman federalized was my Twenty-eighth Division from Pennsylvania.

"At the time, I was a premed student, and I could have gotten a deferment. But I decided that I did not wish to be deferred. Instead, I was promoted to the rank of master sergeant."

Kim's language abilities and knowledge of Asian politics led to his being assigned to military intelligence, and later the Central Intelligence Agency. He served with the CIA in Japan through the Korean War. In 1955 Kim volunteered for the Special Forces, becoming a member of the famous Green Berets.

"I joined the Green Berets because it was the army's elite unconventional warfare unit," he explains. "I believe in unconventional warfare because I thought that was the type of war that America would have to fight more and more in the future."

Kim's subsequent Special Forces assignments took him to various posts in America, and then to Germany following the Berlin Airlift. His tour of duty in Germany completed, Kim, then a young captain, was sent to the army's Command and General Staff College at Fort Leavenworth, Kansas. Following graduation, Kim volunteered for duty with Special Forces in Vietnam.

His service in Vietnam led to a post at the Pentagon, a promotion to the rank of lieutenant colonel, and the opportunity to train other people to fight the kinds of unconventional warfare he believed were so important.

In 1971 Kim would retire from the military after serving a quarter of a century. At the same time, his faith in America and his sense of personal calling in life would be severely challenged.

THE UNRAVELING OF AMERICA

If he had wanted to, Kim could have remained in the military on a fast track to promotion and schooling at one of the military's war colleges, but he chose to leave the service.

By the 1960s and 1970s, things had started to change in America. Domestically the Watergate scandal of the early 1970s shook Americans' faith in their political leaders and institutions.

Meanwhile, the war in Vietnam dragged on. And events like the 1968 My Lai massacre of 347 unarmed men, women, and children fueled a growing antiwar sentiment back home.

"By this time, I had begun to experience some disillusionment," says Kim. "Everything in America was unraveling, it seemed. So many young people were dying in Vietnam, but for what?"

Kim had been overseas so long that he didn't know how tumultuous things were in America. That changed when he came home in 1971.

"As soon as I got off the airplane in my full military regalia and walked through the terminal to hail a cab, I could see the attitudes of people back here.

"I had been fighting overseas for my country and came back to a nation—or more specifically a younger generation—that hated us so."

Kim's career in the U.S. military came to an end. The only problem was, he didn't quite know what he was going to do next.

A HIGHER CALLING

In Okinawa an Episcopal bishop named Edmond Browning asked Kim if he had ever thought about going to seminary and studying for the priesthood.

"Dick, what are you going to do?" asked Browning.

Kim had never considered such a step and told Browning so.

"I never really thought about entering the priesthood," said Kim. "I'm not worthy of such a high calling."

Browning's response was firm and direct: "So, Dick, who do you think you are, God? God will determine whether or not you are worthy."

As he thought about Browning's questions, the calling to become a priest in the church began to settle in.

"I had always wanted to be of service to people," he says. "I had wanted to be a doctor or a social worker, but never considered the priesthood."

In the end Kim decided to leave it up to God. Or as he said at the time, "If it is to be, it will be."

When he announced to his Special Forces command in Okinawa that he was leaving the service to enter seminary at the University of the South, Sewanee, Tennessee, his command sergeant major, out of concern for his well-being, called him aside and asked: "Sir, are you all right?"

He was just fine, and within months, he was attending seminary, where he was introduced not only to theological training but also to a heavy dose of liberal politics.

"I found myself in a community that included a lot of draft dodgers," says Kim. "I think it's legitimate for someone of faith to be a conscientious objector, but these guys were past that.

"At one of our get-acquainted gatherings at seminary, an upperclassman turned to me and asked, 'Dick, are you here to atone for your military sins?'

"'Heck, no,' I told him. 'I have no regrets.'"

Finishing his studies, Kim was ordained to the diaconate in 1973 and to the priesthood in 1974.

Once again, his life's journey was about to move in some interesting new directions. After serving as the assistant chaplain at the University of Alabama in Tuscaloosa, Kim was the rector of parishes in Sheffield, Alabama; Maui, Hawaii; Lexington, Michigan; and finally Detroit, where he served for a decade at St. John's Episcopal Church.

But by that time, Kim felt that the Episcopal Church was unraveling just as America had done during the 1960s and 1970s.

STILL FIGHTING

Kim believes that some of the church leadership at that time embraced women's ordination and even supported the homosexual agenda. To Kim, those decisions seemed to be on the basis of equal rights rather than on the basis of sound biblical teaching or the long tradition and history of the church.

"Bishops were ordaining gay priests. There was a gay priest who actually said that Mother Teresa would have been a better nun if she had had sex. That's the kind of thing that was going on."

Some Episcopalians didn't understand the nature of the changes sweeping over the church. Others didn't care. But Kim was part of a group that was deeply concerned about the consequences of drifting away from biblical moorings to a more relativistic approach.

"Some of us became active in trying to reverse things," states Kim, who was never one to lie down and surrender when he faced opposition.

Initially Kim worked with groups of concerned church leaders who tried to remain within the institution and seek its reform and renewal. In 1991 a group founded an organization called Concerned Clergy and Laity of the Episcopal Church and published a newspaper, *Pro Fide* (For the Faith).

But during the 1990s, there was little that conservatives like Kim found agreeable in the Episcopal Church. "There was a lot of rhetoric, but no action," he observes.

By 1998 many were convinced that efforts to reform the church from within were futile, so they left to form a new organization, the Anglican Mission in America, which has the support of Anglican leaders in other parts of the world who share Kim's concern for the liberal direction of the U.S. church.

People who have known Kim for long won't be surprised at his willingness to fight for what he believes is right. In fact, even though he is now in his seventies, Kim still resembles the brave teenager who left the comforts of home and family in China to strike out into the unknown for the sake of a concept called freedom.

Kim doesn't believe that any country—or any religious organization—is perfect. Yet he's convinced that there is a wellspring of changeless values and beliefs that should form the basis of all we do in life.

"I am standing for the kinds of things America has always stood for, the kinds of things America has always believed," he says. "There are values and beliefs that hold strong, and those aren't changing."

Free at last. Korean Richard Kim left Shanghai, China, after his adopted land was invaded by the Japanese and torn asunder by fighting between Nationalist and Communist troops. When he arrived in Free China, his life began anew.

Serving the Allies. By late 1944, 17-year-old Kim had lied about his age to become a U.S. Army staff sergeant. He served at the Allied headquarters in China.

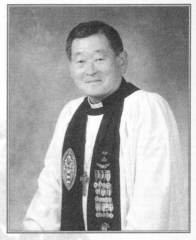

A distinguished career. In 1955, Kim volunteered for the Special Forces, becoming a member of the famous Green Berets. He served the Special Forces in Germany and Vietnam and later received a posting at the Pentagon.

From the military to the ministry. After two decades of military service, Richard Kim followed another calling. "I laid down the crossed rifles of an airborne infantry officer in the Green Berets to pick up the cross of Jesus," he says.

SIXTEEN

MARVIN SMITH

SAVED BY LOVE

Much has been made of the fervent faith of the men who fought in World War II. Many of the stories written about the war talk about the combination of piety and patriotism that inspired millions of seemingly unremarkable people to engage in acts of bravery and even heroism.

Some of the best-known slogans of the period illustrate this wartime religiosity: "Praise the Lord and pass the ammunition," "God is my copilot," and "There are no atheists in foxholes."

Clearly not all U.S. soldiers were card-carrying, Bible-reading, hymn-singing, churchgoing Christians, but many veterans experienced things during the war that led to profound life changes and a deepening spiritual sensitivity.

U.S. Army Captain Marvin Smith is one such veteran. A participant in the massive Normandy invasion force that fought its way across northern France, Smith found himself in plenty of tight spots. He was even wounded during the furious fighting at Saint-Lô, an ancient fortress town that was the site of an important German stronghold.

Ultimately it was love that saved Smith. It was God's love—not battlefield fear—that inspired Smith to commit his life to Christ after the war. And it was his deep love for his wife, Virginia—a love that warmed his heart across a distance of thousands of miles—that sustained him during some of the war's darkest moments.

MEMORIES OF LOVE AND LOSS

People used to call World War II veterans the silent generation. Many who had survived the war returned home determined to get on with their lives and do what they could to put the past behind them, including their memories of war.

But Marvin Smith was different. In 1985 he wrote down his memories in a self-published booklet, *The Hedgerows of Normandy: A Soldier's Memoir.* In the booklet he explained his reasons for writing about his experiences.

"Why should I record events of my World War II days?" he asked.

Certainly not to preserve them in my memory, for they are etched forever.

Perhaps it is to let others know what we experienced there . . . I leave no legacy of fame to cause others to desire my story. Perhaps it is, at long last, to empty myself of long constrained emotions of experiences.

I do not know whether I can tell everything and may tell things I shouldn't. Frankly, many of my thoughts and feelings shocked and surprised me. I shall record events that produced in me laughter, tears, fear, pride, courage, and all other emotions that one can experience.

Smith dedicated the memoir to "my beloved wife Virginia whose love and support sustained me." And in the pages of the memoir, Smith gives a disarmingly honest account of both the terrors of battle and the deep love he had for his wife.

Smith was born December 27, 1918, and was raised on a wheat

and cattle farm near Haviland, Kansas. Life was hard, but the family was close.

"They believed in hard work, and they believed in working their sons too," he recalls.

"My parents went to church for funerals and weddings. They were good people and better than a lot of people who talked a lot about religion. My brother and I went to Sunday school a few times when neighbors asked us to."

Smith's parents passed on a love for America that encouraged him to enlist in the army and attend Officer Candidate School.

"America had passed the draft law, and all young people my age were to be drafted for one year of military service," he explains.

"With war looming, I found out that by volunteering instead of being drafted, I could select my unit, even my job. I hoped I could get my year over with, so that I would be free to marry or go into business, possibly in bookkeeping or accounting."

As it turned out, Smith would be in the service much longer than one year. But he has no regrets.

"I don't consider it a mistake at all," he says. "I think I did the right thing."

Virginia Dell Cook was born in Independence, Missouri, on August 7, 1917, to parents who were committed Christians and who passed that faith on to their daughter.

"My father was a deacon emeritus in the Baptist church," she says. "I grew up learning about God. The church held an evangelistic service when I was eight, and I went forward, accepted Christ, and was baptized."

Virginia attended business college, which gave her the knowledge she needed to land a job in Martinez, California, working for the county auditor of Contra Costa County. Soon after America entered World War II, the area was flooded with U.S. servicemen.

"I met Marvin right after Pearl Harbor," she says. "The girls in the county office had a party in January 1942 for some of the soldiers who had just moved in. I met Marvin the first night he got to California."

Four months later, the two were married.

"It was a whirlwind romance," she recalls. "We had two years of weekends together. I followed from town to town, finding a room, as he moved from camp to camp for intensive training. One year we moved thirteen times. We made many friends, an experience that made life very happy in spite of the hardships. And it lasted."

In February 1944, as Marvin's division was leaving Camp Atterbury, Indiana, Virginia set out for Missouri; Marvin's next stop was the port of embarkation in preparation for the D-Day invasions.

"I held her in my arms," wrote Marvin, "and with the last kiss bid her an optimistic farewell. I marveled at her courage—the way she held up at the last good-bye."

But Virginia wouldn't have described herself as courageous.

"No, I felt sad," she recalls, "but you have to do what you have to do."

Like many other military couples who were hugging and saying good-bye that day, Marvin and Virginia hoped for the best, but they were prepared for the worst. He had given her power of attorney that would allow her to take charge of their business affairs if he never returned.

"I was optimistic," she says, "but I was also afraid he would be killed, which was a realistic fear. More than half of the men in the company he had trained with for more than two years never came home."

Following their fond farewell, Captain Smith and the men he commanded in Company K boarded the USS *Argentina* troop ship for the long journey across the Atlantic.

When he had a chance, Smith went up to the deck to survey the scene. What he saw was the largest military armada to ever cross the Atlantic. And his ship was in the "graveyard" position at the rear of the convoy, making it a prime target for enemy submarines.

Preparing for Invasion

The convoy made it across the ocean, and the USS *Argentina* docked in Glasgow, Scotland, where it unloaded its men, who were transported by train to southern England, "just a few miles from the Nazis on the coast of France."

Conditions in camp were cold and damp, and many of the men struggled with their feelings of love and longing for their faraway wives.

"We could not build fires due to the scarcity of fuel, so we wore over-coats even in billets," he wrote. "We were hungry all the time."

At night as the men tried to sleep, they could hear air-raid sirens in the distance and the sound of German planes flying low overhead.

Though food was scarce, liquor was plentiful, and some men made a habit of visiting local pubs, where they could drink away their sorrows and mix with local women.

"There was a lonely void in our hearts," wrote Smith, who wrote often to his wife. "It was good to be near women in the pubs and to just hear their voices."

Some men went farther than merely listening to the women talk, but not Smith. "I longed for my wife and was extremely lonely for her," he wrote. "I was sad and had low morale."

About the only things that made life bearable for Smith were Virginia's letters and photos of his wife that he had brought with him. But soon, the discomforts of camp life would be replaced by the anxieties of battle.

Many people think of the Normandy invasions as synonymous with D-Day. But June 6, 1944, was only the launch date of that massive Allied invasion that would involve American, British, and Canadian troops and would stretch over a period of weeks.

Smith knew when the invasions had begun because he could hear hundreds of Allied fighter and bomber planes flying over his location on their way to the French coastline.

Company K was to be a part of a later influx. "My first real fear came as we were briefed on a large-scale map showing our landing area, and that the enemy opposing us would likely be the 40th Panzer Division," wrote Smith.

"The word *Panzer* was the dreaded name for enemy tanks and armored cars. I dreaded these steel monsters, which could fire machine guns and larger armor-piercing shells directly into your foxhole."

Six days after D-Day, it was time for Smith's Company K to head out for Utah Beach. Most of the Allied casualties had already been removed from the beaches, but the surrounding shores were littered with the remains of wrecked ships and other debris.

By that time German forces had already been cleared from the beach areas. The job facing Smith's company was to press inland, forcing enemy troops farther and farther inland. The fighting would test Smith's character and deepen his longing for his wife.

WAGING A DEADLY GROUND WAR

Smith's 180 men marched in the evening darkness, dodging bullets from enemy snipers, and standing as still as statues when German planes dropped flares that lit up the night and exposed the troops to enemy fire.

There was a moment of comic relief when a bald sergeant had his helmet blown off the top of his head by enemy fire. The sergeant survived, but without his helmet his shiny head made "an excellent target for the enemy to spot."

But most of the time, there was little anyone could do to break the tension and the ever-present reminders of death. Smith still recalls the time he saw a dead U.S. soldier, who had a bullet hole in his forehead.

"Death could come to any of us at any time," he realized with a shocking finality. "How different the dead looked compared to the dead at a funeral back home."

The men made their way across the French countryside, dodging machine gunners, attacking enemy lines, and jumping over German foxholes, shooting soldiers hiding there as they jumped. Soldiers also faced the constant threat of friendly fire as Allied artillery shells went off target and landed dangerously close to their own troops.

It was while Company K was making its slow progress across the landscape that Smith made a decision that has haunted him ever since.

Coming across a dead German soldier, Smith dispatched a loyal and efficient sergeant to search the dead man for documents about German troop movements.

"Search him, but be careful," said Smith. But barely had the sergeant made his way to the corpse before he was shot dead by a hidden German sniper. The death of a soldier who was following his orders shocked Smith and reminded him anew of the responsibilities of his rank.

FROM VIRE TO SAINT-LÔ

One of the company's most dangerous assignments was to rout enemy troops from the Vire canal crossing, which had been a strategic location for the Germans and was equally important to advancing Allied troops. There Smith's fear grew.

"I had not prayed to God before because I felt that it wasn't right to have nothing to do with God previously and then suddenly in battle start calling on Him," wrote Smith.

"I thought it was very poor taste, and that God would not have anything to do with me. But fear won out. I prayed, 'Oh, God, if there is a God, please protect us now as we go into the enemy area in this darkness. Help us now, oh, God!'"

As it turned out, Company K walked silently on the one-mile trek to the canal and, upon arriving at their destination, faced no opposition.

"Could it be that God had answered my prayer?" he wondered. It was a question he couldn't answer, but he doesn't recall praying again during the war.

Instead, he found comfort in a newly arrived photo of Virginia, which held an honored spot on an earthen shelf in the wall of his freshly dug foxhole.

"Out of the picture she spoke to me," says Smith, "conveying love, trust, and confidence."

Virginia adds that she believes her prayers made a difference. "We had a slogan," she says. "Whenever we kissed good-bye or hello throughout courtship and marriage, Marvin and I always said, 'We never miss!' I was praying for him the whole time, and I never gave up."

K Company crossed the River Vire, moved to the town of Saint-Jean-de-Daye, and then marched into enemy-held territory and the town of Saint-Lô.

The picturesque town was a strategic rail center for all of northern France. That's why the Germans considered control of the town so important. And that's why Allied troops wanted to capture it, thus loosening up the "Normandy bottleneck," which had limited movement of Allied troops.

Enemy soldiers defended Saint-Lô for two months as part of what an Associated Press reporter called "the hardest American clash with the Germans in the Battle for France." But Allied troops continued to punish the town, reducing many of its historic buildings to piles of rubble.

The men of K Company were part of the assault, and soon Smith found himself hunkered down in a foxhole trying to find a way to attack an enemy tank that was barricaded behind a French house. But an incoming mortar shell changed his plans.

"I was hit," he recalls. "There was a chunk missing out of my right wrist. Blood was spurting out of my wrist in a stream that was an inch or two high, and I knew that I was hit bad."

Smith grabbed his wrist in an effort to stop the bleeding. And instead of waiting for medical personnel to evacuate him to the rear, he walked out.

"Rather than remaining in a position where I was like a sitting duck, I made my way out," he says.

He was soon picked up by a jeep that was taking wounded to an aid station.

"I groaned as soon as I was in the jeep, but someone said, 'Be quiet and look at that poor guy above you on the stretcher.' He was in much worse shape than I was.

"When I got to the aid station, they told me I had a severed artery and a damaged thumb tendon and nerves. All they could do for me was give me drugs. Frankly I was just glad to be alive."

Soon Smith was on a plane to England and a military hospital. Through a window, he could hear the voices of children playing in a nearby playground.

"It was like heaven," he says. "I just loved their soft, innocent voices."

But the voice he most wanted to hear was that of his beloved Virginia.

"One night I dreamed she was walking down the aisle by my bed, and I was in ecstasy," he wrote. "But I awoke, and it was only a nurse."

Recovery would require six to eight months, so Smith was shipped back to America. While he was relieved to be heading back to the States, he was also plagued with uncertainties.

"I wanted to go home to see my wife. In fact, I could hardly wait. But I also wanted to rejoin my beloved K Company. I thought I needed to be there helping them. I felt guilty being in a hospital, while not serving them."

HOMEWARD BOUND

It seemed to take forever for the ship that carried Smith and other wounded and returning soldiers to reach America. Along the way, he bumped into Bing Crosby, who was returning from entertaining the troops.

"We spoke when we met," says Smith. "He always seemed to be humming a tune or whistling. He cared about the fighting men, and here he was on this ship when he didn't have to be there. There was some risk on that ship from submarines, and I was somewhat impressed at his dedication."

When he got to land, Smith fell to the ground: "It was a great feeling." And he hurriedly bought and drank bottles of milk, his first taste of the real thing after months of a powdered substitute.

"Oh, man. That was one thing I really wanted when I got back here."

He also wanted to see Virginia.

"I spotted her, and after a long embrace and kisses, we walked to our hotel room! It was like a dream! I had imagined all kinds of bad things that could happen to her on her way to meet me—a bus wreck or a train wreck. But here she was with tears, meeting me. I had lived! I had her again! I can't describe it all!"

Smith brought his injured arm, a Purple Heart, and a Bronze Star back from Europe and went to Springfield, Missouri, for treatment and operations. Both guilt and memories of battle continued to plague him.

"Here I was with my wife in safe, warm comfort while my comrades fought and died in zero weather and snow and ice in Europe," he says.

"And at nights I would awaken to the slamming together of freight train cars, which sounded like shells crashing, and I was again on the battlefield!"

But soon, life settled into a comfortable regularity. "Life was wonderful with her, and combat memories began to fade," he says.

Marvin and Virginia made up for lost time, starting a new life together as a family and rapidly having three children. It was in these happy circumstances that Smith would finally give his life to a God that he hadn't been sure had existed while he was in the face of battle.

Virginia had been attending church throughout the war, and after the children were born, she took them with her. One morning, their oldest daughter, Carol, approached her father and said, "Daddy, I wish you could go to Sunday school with me." The invitation grabbed Smith's heart.

"She had on a pretty dress, black shiny shoes, and white stockings up to her knees. She was cute as a bug. She was so precious to me, and I loved her so much.

"After a night of pondering her request, I could find no logical excuse. I had promised her I would go next Sunday. In the middle of the night I had told God I was ready to follow Him."

But before he went to church the next Sunday, Smith paid a visit to the preacher at Pratt Baptist Church in Pratt, Kansas.

"I went up to the preacher's office, and I told him my circumstances. I said, 'I'm tired of swimming around in life and going the wrong way.' I told him I wanted to become a Christian, and I wanted to be a believer, and that's why I was visiting him at church.

"He explained what would happen the following Sunday at church, and when that day came, I went forward and accepted Christ with tears in my eyes. I was baptized, and since then, I have lived as consistent a Christian life as I possibly can."

Now living in Sisters, Oregon, the Smiths remain involved in their local church.

RETURNING TO THE SCENE OF BATTLE

Marvin Smith has returned to France three times since the war as part of veteran tours of war areas. In 1984, he took Virginia with him for the fortieth anniversary of D-Day. In 1989, the couple took their three children with them for an emotional tour of sites where Marvin had fought. And in 1994, Marvin was on hand for the D-Day fiftieth anniversary celebration. Each time, he had plenty of chances to reflect on the war and its impact on his life.

"One thing that impressed me about the war was that I was not as frightened as I thought I would be when I got in dangerous situations," he says. "I also think it made me appreciate life itself and made me want to live life more fully."

A ride before fighting. Captain Marvin Smith rides a bike in England before he and his men from K Company invaded the beaches of Normandy.

Making up for lost time. After the war, the Smiths focused on family and faith.

Battered Saint-Lô. Not much was left of the historic town of Saint-Lô after two months of intense fighting. The battle also left Smith with an injury that would end his service in the war.

SEVENTEEN

EARL CLARK

A HIGHER LOVE

After summer is long gone and fall leaves are buried under mounds of snow, many people head indoors where they hide like hibernating bears from the ravages of winter swirling outside their frosty windows.

Not Earl Clark, who loves few things in life more than feeling the chill of the breeze and hearing the swoosh of the snow as he glides down one of the world's many snow-capped mountains.

Clark is in his early eighties, but he and his wife, Betty, still ski more than fifty times a year. And to hear him talk about it, the activity is close to a religious experience.

"For years and years, I have loved being in the mountains," he says. "First came climbing and the thrill of reaching the summit of great peaks. Then came nearly seventy years of skiing.

"I have so loved the mountains. I feel that they are a part of God's majestic creation, and I feel that Betty and I are privileged to be able to enjoy them in the way that we do. We have enjoyed the high mountains together for our entire married life."

During World War II, he was part of an elite group of skiing soldiers who were able to combine their love of the great outdoors with military service in the Tenth Mountain Division, a specialized unit that saw more than its share of fighting and death in both the Pacific and the European theaters.

After the war was over, Clark and many other veterans of the Tenth were instrumental in creating America's ski industry, which is now a multibillion-dollar powerhouse.

But Clark first fell in love with skiing as a teenager, when it represented a positive alternative to the tragedies that had befallen his family.

From Preacher's Kid to Eagle Scout

Clark's parents met in Massachusetts while both were students at Gordon Theological Seminary, where his father was preparing to be a pastor. After they graduated, they moved to South Londonderry, Vermont.

"It was my father's first little Methodist church located in a tiny community," says Clark. "And that's the town where I was born."

Soon, the family moved to a series of churches in small towns in upstate Wisconsin. By then the Great Depression had hit. Members of small churches across the country were unable to continue putting their donations into the offering basket, and many pastors were forced to look for new ways to support their families.

"At that time, my father left the ministry, and once that happened, my mother and I felt he would never go back to it. It was too embarrassing for him, financially and otherwise."

Before long, Clark's father abandoned the family and totally disappeared.

"At that point I was eleven years old. My mother and I went to Chicago and moved in with an uncle."

Clark felt that his world had ended. He had to fend for himself in an entirely new environment. Into that void walked Arthur Kramer, a Chicago Boy Scout leader who became a surrogate father for Clark and exposed him to the great outdoors.

"We were having a very tough time," says Clark. "Then Arthur Kramer and two other Boy Scout leaders took me by the hand and introduced me to skiing, camping, and everything else. These three young men played a major role in my life.

"They helped me become an Eagle Scout. And as I look back on it now, it's clear that achieving the rank of Eagle Scout led to most of the positive things that happened in my life beyond that point."

Just about every pastime has its early adopters—those people who latch on to it long before anyone else does. When it came to skiing, Clark was an early adopter.

The sport began in Europe, where people had enjoyed mountain activities and sports for centuries. During the early 1930s, some Ivy League colleges hired Austrian, German, and Swiss ski coaches and participated in some of the first intercollegiate skiing competitions. And in 1936, a world-famous ski resort opened at Sun Valley, Idaho.

At that time, the sport attracted affluent, educated, cosmopolitan people, not poor kids like Clark. Still, after he was introduced to skiing in 1932, Clark took to it with abandon.

"I had begun skiing on toe-strap skis with galoshes serving as ski boots, and as the years went by, I graduated to better equipment, including hickory skis and real ski boots.

"At first I would ski near the Chicago area. Then in the summers of 1939, 1940, and 1941, I took a leave of absence from my employer and went to the Grand Teton National Park in Wyoming. This led to a lot of climbing and skiing."

But by 1941, the sounds of war were echoing around the globe, and Clark could hear them even high up in his beloved mountains.

MOUNTAIN SOLDIERS

When Clark realized that he might be able to serve Uncle Sam in the great outdoors, he jumped at the chance.

"By the fall of 1941, I learned through friends in the American Alpine Club that the United States might be creating a special army unit focused on skiing and mountaineering," he says.

"By this time the draft was taking place. I knew that being single and twenty-three, some time in the military was certainly ahead of me, so this unit was the obvious place for me."

He applied to the unit immediately, but it wasn't until after the attack on Pearl Harbor that he was actually inducted. On St. Patrick's Day in March 1942, he reported for duty. Several months later he was sent to Fort Benning, Georgia, where after officer training, he became a second lieutenant. He was assigned to a unit that would later become the Tenth Mountain Division.

Things got off to a rough start for his unit. The Eighty-seventh Mountain Infantry Regiment was assigned to take part in an amphibious assault on Kiska Island, one of two tiny islands in the Aleutian group, which stretched from the tip of Alaska across the northern Pacific.

In 1942 the Japanese had occupied Kiska and Attu, two bleak, rocky, and remote specks of land. America wanted them back and began bombing them. In 1943 the amphibious assault on Kiska was supposed to conclude the American efforts. But when troops landed, including members of the Eighty-seventh Regiment, they discovered that the Japanese had already left!

Such escapades might seem humorous, but the assault in the Aleutians was tragic too. More than three hundred men were lost, including the crew of a destroyer that hit an enemy mine.

The Tenth Mountain Division spent the winter of 1943–44 training at Colorado's Camp Hale. Located some 9,400 feet up in the Rocky

Mountains, the camp was certainly one of the most unusual and challenging training facilities U.S. troops had ever seen.

The facility was abandoned soon after war's end, in part because it was so difficult to get to and so expensive to maintain. Today, all one sees at the site is some of the partial remains of building foundations. But when Clark was there, the camp was full of people and activity.

At its peak, the Tenth Mountain Division had nearly fifteen thousand men, and thousands of them trained at Camp Hale, honing their skiing skills as well as learning how to maneuver and fight in mountainous terrain, how to climb cliffs and rappel back down while carrying heavy weapons and backpacks, and how to survive for extended periods of time in subzero temperatures.

"It was our common love of the mountains that was the glue that held the men of the Tenth Mountain Division together so completely," says Clark.

"Unlike members of so many units in the army, who had just the army, we had a great love of the mountains, which kept us together before, during, and after the war."

By late 1944, the division was on its way to Italy, where both its unity and its mountaineering skills would be put to the ultimate test in the Apennine Mountains.

ATTACKING THE GOTHIC LINE

By 1944, German forces were stretched to the breaking point as they fended off counteroffensives in Russia, North Africa, and Europe.

In June, Allied forces had recaptured Rome. Afterward, German troops moved to the Northern Apennine Mountains just north of the Arno River Valley and the city of Florence. There they hunkered down behind their so-called "Gothic Line." The line, which stretched across Italy from the Tyrrhenian Sea in the west to the Adriatic Sea in the east, was heavily fortified, with many of the defenses sited at the top of mountain ridges or peaks.

Clearly that was an assignment for the Tenth Mountain Division, whose men were commanded to go after two of the Germans' key mountain positions. One of the sites was called Riva Ridge, which was located adjacent to the highest mountain of the North Apennines, Mount Belvedere.

The assault on Riva Ridge showcased the division's skill and daring. During a dangerous nighttime attack, nearly one thousand men scaled two-thousand-foot cliffs using ropes and pitons. The sneak attack behind enemy lines was a stunning success, as members of the Tenth surprised and routed German defenders who had held tight against months of Allied attacks.

Now that Mount Belvedere was in Allied hands, Allied troops led by the Tenth could stream into the strategically important Po Valley, pushing German troops ahead of them as they advanced.

Members of the Tenth were the first Allied troops to reach and cross the Po River. In fact, the troops were covering so much ground so quickly that they outran retreating German forces. By war's end, the fast-moving Tenth had captured twenty thousand German prisoners.

Due to such efforts, the Germans in Italy surrendered before their comrades in the north. But such success didn't come without cost. During 122 straight days of combat, the Tenth suffered five thousand casualties, including nearly one thousand killed.

"The fighting was tough, but I was content," says Clark. "I was where I wanted to be, and I was serving with a unit I wanted to be with."

Clark also felt that God had been watching out for him, keeping him safe while others around him perished.

"During all this fighting, I never so much as scratched a knuckle," he says.

"There were circumstances, several in fact, where I just knew that I had been cared for by some divine power. I didn't understand it, but I knew for some reason I was being spared."

Christianity had been a difficult subject for Clark since his preacher-father ran out on the family. But two things helped to change that during Clark's war years. One was a devout officer who earned Clark's respect and trust.

"I had a regimental commander who was a totally involved Christian man," explains Clark. "After we had three of our chaplains killed when an aid station blew up, the commander conducted our worship services. This was quite unusual, and he became a very dear friend. Our friendship continued for many years after the war."

Clark also had a chance encounter with his father.

"I was checking into a hotel, and my father was checking in at the same instant," says Clark, who walked to his father and said, "'Do you know me?' This was years after he had left us. It had taken me many years to do so, but with the help of my faith I had forgiven him completely. There was no longer anger or bitterness there. But how weird the circumstances were!"

After the war, Clark went back to Chicago. But having tasted the beauty of Colorado while training at Camp Hale, he felt he had to return to the state's lofty mountains.

He moved to Colorado in the summer of 1946, and by the end of the year he was in charge of the ski patrol at the recently opened Arapahoe Basin resort. He wasn't the only former member of the Tenth to participate in the U.S. ski industry's postwar boom years.

"There were sixty-two ski areas in the U.S. that were either developed or operated by veterans of the Tenth Mountain Division," he says.

In some cases the veterans left reminders of their war service at the resorts they founded. At Vail, for example, one of the runs is named Riva Ridge.

A New Life

It was in Colorado that Clark found Betty, who would still be his wife and skiing partner more than fifty years later. She would help introduce him to a deeper expression of the Christian faith than he had experienced thus far in life.

"She was the daughter of a Lutheran minister, and after we married, we became Presbyterians," he says. "We were active churchgoers in the early years of our marriage.

"In time Betty became more and more involved in a ministry called Young Life, which works with young people. As part of one of the programs she was involved in, we were invited to go up to the ministry's mountain facility called Trail West for a weekend. As we were there with other husbands and wives, I really turned a corner in my understanding of God.

"Later my faith continued to grow at a men's Bible study group, which met at the Cherry Hills Country Club in Denver.

"One day I went to lunch with one of the Young Life program directors. I asked him when lightning was going to strike. I felt that I was certainly ready to really turn my life over to Christ, but thought that had to happen in some kind of dramatic way.

"He picked up a teaspoon and handed it to me. Then he asked me a question.

"'Any lightning yet?' he asked.

"I looked at him, uncertain what he meant. Then he explained.

"'You've been offered a gift. You don't need any lightning bolts. Just take it.'

"Since that very moment, I knew that I was a Christian."

Today, Clark remains active in a weekly men's Bible study group. He has also served as an elder in his local congregation, which is a member of the Evangelical Presbyterian Church, and has served his denomination in various capacities as well. In addition he has donated countless hours to groups such as Young Life, the Boy Scouts, Junior Achievement, and the Denver Chamber of Commerce.

But he also remained involved in matters related to skiing and veterans of his beloved Tenth Mountain Division. Many veterans of the Tenth had returned to Colorado after the war, and for years Clark served as the president of their Rocky Mountain Chapter. But in 1971 he thought it would be better to create a truly national association: "As they always say, if you don't like the cooking, you become the cook."

From 1971 to 1978 he served as the association's first national president. He was also instrumental in forming a group called the International Federation of Mountain Soldiers, which brought veterans of the Tenth together with their peers from Germany, Austria, France, and Italy.

And in the late 1980s and early 1990s, Clark served as president of the Over the Hill Gang, International, an adventure club for seniors that regularly visits some of the world's most renowned ski resorts.

Among all the awards and honors Clark has received, one that he appreciates the most is his induction into the Colorado Ski Hall of Fame. It may not sound as prestigious as being a member of the U.S. Army Hall of Fame, which is one of his other honors, but being part of the Ski Hall of Fame means he can ski for free. It's a benefit he uses quite frequently during the long winter season.

THE TENTH LIVES AGAIN

The Tenth Mountain Division was deactivated after World War II, only to be briefly reactivated during the 1950s. Then after decades of inaction, the division was reactivated once again in 1985. Since then it has been deployed in numerous actions in places like Somalia and Haiti.

In 2001, American troops were called to Uzbekistan to fight against terrorists in Afghanistan who had been sheltered there by the Taliban government. Once again, it was the Tenth that was called to perform some of the most delicate fighting in the country's remote mountain regions.

The division's newfound celebrity, combined with a resurgence of patriotism and renewed interest in World War II, means that Clark is making more presentations than usual about the division's history and accomplishments.

During Veterans Day observances in 2001, he gave a slide presentation and talk to nearly four hundred interested senior-high-school students.

"The whole school was bedecked in flags," says Clark. "I was thrilled to death to see the flags flying. The attitude of the American people is like it was after Pearl Harbor. We've been hit, and it's time to roll up our sleeves and prove what we are."

Clark's memories of World War II are fond ones.

"Unlike some who served, I found the army to be an exciting and rewarding experience in my life," he says.

"I had come from a pretty impoverished type of situation, but after I enlisted in the army, all of a sudden I was an officer. Over time, I rose in rank, and I was a captain when the unit was deactivated after the war. My life had made a major positive turn."

Clark stayed in the active reserve until he retired in 1979. By that time, he was a lieutenant colonel, and his military career had served him well.

Thinking back, Clark considers his service in the military one of the three major events in shaping his life.

"If it had not been for World War II, those three Boy Scout leaders in Chicago, and my faith in God, who knows what would have become of Earl Clark?" he asks.

But he doesn't have time to reflect any longer. It's a December day in Colorado. The sun is shining brightly. The air is clear and crisp. And the mountains are covered with a foot of fresh snow.

That means it's time for Earl and Betty Clark to put on their skis and hit the slopes!

Military mountaineers. *Young men like Earl Clark combined patriotism with a love for mountaineering, serving in the Tenth Mountain Division, a specialized unit that fought in both the Pacific and European theaters.*

Rocky Mountain high. *Earl Clark is now in his 80s, but he and his wife, Betty, still ski more than 50 times a year. "I have so loved the mountains," he says. "I feel that they are a part of God's majestic creation."*

EIGHTEEN

THOMAS PRUDHOMME

SEEING MIRACLES
AT CLOSE RANGE

Thomas Prudhomme has been a true-blue American for most of his eighty-one years.

"I always have been a patriot all my life," says the Louisiana resident in his distinct Natchitoches drawl.

"When I was a kid, we were living in Washington, D.C., and I remember the Fourth of July celebrations, complete with fireworks and a band playing John Philip Sousa. And the American flag has always been a wonderful thing to me. I've been hanging a flag outside my house twenty-four hours a day for at least fifty years."

Though small, the flag has a prominent spot: it hangs from a metal carport and is lit by a bright garage light. Over the past half century, Louisiana's blustery weather has taken its toll on these flags, but not to worry. "When one gets bad, I get another one," he announces.

Few episodes in American history have generated as strong an outpouring of patriotism as the outbreak of World War II. In the 1940s, thousands and thousands of American boys enlisted in the military, determined to do their part to fight for liberty overseas.

But Thomas Prudhomme (pronounced PRUDE-um) was not one of the volunteers. He waited until October 1941, when he was drafted.

"As I jokingly tell people, sure, I volunteered. The sheriff came to the door and said, 'You're drafted.' And I said, 'OK. I'm coming. I'm coming.'"

During basic training at Camp Shelby in Mississippi, Prudhomme was determined to take the path of least resistance. When a man came through the camp recruiting volunteers for the Army Air Corps, Prudhomme declined, while his buddy Paul Keyser readily accepted the offer.

"You had to sign up for two years," recalls Prudhomme. "I said, 'Not me. I'm only going to be in this army one year.'"

It would be a fateful decision. "Paul went to Florida, and I went to hell and back," he states.

Within a year, Prudhomme would volunteer to become a member of the First Ranger Battalion, a U.S. Army special-service unit patterned after the British force's elite Commandos. Known for staging surprise raids behind enemy lines, the Rangers went into battle knowing that there was a darn good chance they wouldn't come back alive.

Prudhomme's service in the Rangers was more dangerous than the work his buddy Paul faced in the Air Corps, but the excitement attracted him to the elite unit. His service also lasted longer than he had expected.

"I served the army for three years, eight months, two days, and one-half hour," he says.

During this period, Prudhomme was involved in some of the most deadly skirmishes of the war. And along the way, he saw his courage grow, his faith in God deepen, and his friendships with his fellow fighting men blossom.

"A lot of things that might have otherwise bothered me don't bother me any longer because any of the stuff going on now can't be as terrifying as being a combat soldier."

War also gave Prudhomme numerous chances to witness the miracle-working power of God at close range.

"My being here today is a miracle," he emphasizes. "My life has been a whole series of miracles. I wouldn't have survived everything I did without the help of the Lord."

FROM GOLDBRICK TO RANGER

During his time with the Rangers, Prudhomme was a dedicated, hard-working soldier. But prior to joining the elite group, he didn't earn any medals for his dedication or hard work. "Basically I was an expert at getting out of doing stuff," he says. "They called me the goldbrick."

That term isn't used much today, so two definitions from the *World Book Dictionary* might be helpful:

a) to avoid duties by any evasion or excuse, such as pretended illness;
b) a person, especially in the army or navy, who avoids duty or shirks work.

And as far as Prudhomme could tell, the army seemed to be involved in its own comedy of errors. Two examples tell the story.

"I was in infantry basic training at Camp Croft in South Carolina when an officer told me, 'You qualify for signal school.' That's where I learned Morse code and how to use signal flags. But when they shipped a big trainload of us to Fort Dix, New Jersey, there was a mix-up. A master sergeant at the depot asked, 'Where did you guys come from?' Apparently they did not know that a couple hundred soldiers were coming his way.

"I wound up in the Thirty-fifth Infantry Division. When I learned that my mother was coming up to Philadelphia to see her sister, I asked the first sergeant if I could have a pass to go see her. After that visit I came back to camp, and the barracks were empty. There was just one boy sitting on his bunk crying. After being trucked around from one place to another, we were transferred to other companies. I had been transferred to the Fifty-third Medical Battalion. I was a bedpan chaser in the hospital."

In March 1942, he arrived in Belfast, Northern Ireland, for further medical training. There, too, he was more interested in fun than fighting.

"One time there was a group of us hanging out in a garden near an old castle. We were shooting dice and playing cards, and if there was any beer around, we were probably drinking beer. Then I saw a colonel approaching. I said, 'Hey, guys, make like you're pulling weeds out of the grass.'

"I stood up and saluted the colonel, who had asked what we were doing. I told him, 'Sir, it looks so bad here that we're getting these guys to pull up these weeds.' He told us to carry on."

Clearly the army provided plenty of opportunities for goofing off if that's what someone wanted to do, but Prudhomme wasn't satisfied with goldbricking.

"I had been trained well," he says. "I could use a rifle or a machine gun. I knew Morse code and telephone installation. And I had received a lot of medical training. I wanted to get this war started instead of sitting around bases doing nothing."

When he heard that the army was going to create the First Ranger Battalion, he told his fellow soldiers, "I'm going to join the Rangers." All the guys who heard him laughed, but the captain who interviewed him wasn't laughing.

"His name was Captain Alva Miller, and I told him I wanted to join the Rangers for the same reasons everyone else did. I had heard about what the British Commandos were doing to carry war to the Germans. I knew what the Commandos had been doing, and I wanted to do it too."

Miller was impressed, selecting Prudhomme to join his elite unit. In time Miller would become a father figure or big brother to the new recruit.

TRAINING FOR TOUGH TIMES

The British Commandos had been formed in June 1940 at a time when the British were unable to mount large-scale frontal attacks against Axis forces. Their goal was to increase their chances of success by applying innovative tactics to the conventional warfare of the day. For the rest of the war, the Commandos would demonstrate their courage and bravery by landing behind enemy lines and paving the way for Allied forces.

America's Rangers were founded with similar goals in mind. Initially receiving training from the British, the all-volunteer Rangers prepared for amphibious assaults and other dangerous operations.

But Prudhomme needed more than a vague commitment to qualify for the Rangers. He needed to pass a grueling ten-day training regimen, or he would be returned to bedpan duty.

"Every morning we lined up and began a terribly strenuous set of exercises," he says. "And every day, an officer would get up and say, 'Today is going to be worse than it was yesterday. If you want to quit, you're welcome to go back to your outfit.'"

On July 1, 1942, Prudhomme was shipped off to Achnacarry Castle, Scotland, for even more intense training with British Commando veterans. There the Rangers learned rock climbing, boat craft, knife fighting, unarmed combat, and survival techniques.

"These were some of the worst exercises I had ever seen. We carried around telephone poles and muscled them into the air. They were running us like the devil. We marched hour after hour, we swam in cold water, we practiced boat landings, and we learned how to navigate collapsible canvas boats."

Some didn't survive the training. One soldier drowned during the swimming exercises while the men were crossing a lake in full equipment. "After that happened, our commander, Major William Darby of Darby's Rangers fame, lined us all up. We were shivering from the cold weather. He said, 'We've had one man drown. Let's not have that happen again.' Then we went back through the whole swimming exercise once again."

Another time, a Ranger was hit with some of the live ammo used in the training. (The precise location of his injuries can be deduced from the nickname the men gave him: "Butts.")

FACING DEATH

The Rangers hadn't even gone into combat yet, and already men were dying and getting injured. That reality, combined with conversations Prudhomme had with British trainers, forced him to face the fact that he might die very soon.

"Everyone knew that he could be dead as soon as we went into combat," he says. "I didn't like that thought, but I knew that when I joined the Rangers, and in a sense I expected it.

"I didn't think about dying every day, but it did change the way I looked at things. For one thing I had a girlfriend back home named Lucille. After a while, I got to the point where I quit writing much of anything in my letters to her. I didn't expect to get home, so I didn't write her love letters. And after a while, I quit writing her anything about what we would do when I got home and we got married because I didn't think that would ever happen."

During those tense days of training in Scotland, Prudhomme met a man who would change his life. His name was Father Albert Basil, and he was a Catholic priest who served as a chaplain to the British Commandos.

Prudhomme had been baptized as a Roman Catholic, but his upbringing wasn't overwhelmingly religious. His father was a Catholic, but his mother was a Methodist.

"I can't say that my parents weren't good Christians, but they were not too hot on going to church," he says. "They raised us kids as Christians, but they just didn't attend church services too much."

Prudhomme's own churchgoing habits were about to change.

"I was in the chaplain's tent shining his shoes, and as I did so, I was cussing under my breath. At that point, the chaplain started interrogating me.

"'Are you a Catholic?' he asked.

"'Yes, I am,' I replied.

"'When was the last time you went to confession?'

"'Well, it's been a couple of years ago.'

"'How many people have you murdered?'

"'I haven't murdered anybody,' I declared.

"'How many churches have you burned down?'

"'I wouldn't burn down no churches,' I said.

"'Well, perhaps you're not so bad after all.'"

It was an odd sort of benediction, but for Prudhomme, it was an introduction into the spiritual practices that provided sustenance for the Rangers.

"If you read some of the history books about the Rangers, you will see all kinds of horrible things in there. Some of these books make it look like we were all jailbirds or something, but we were tough, well-trained people.

"And we had prayers all the time. Whenever everybody gathered up in a bunch, everyone was ready to pray. There weren't any denominations in the Rangers, and I don't know who was Catholic and who wasn't. All I know is that many of us regularly turned to the Lord. You had to. If any of these people weren't Christians, I don't know who they were."

Father Basil was more than a priest. He was a fearless chaplain who walked boldly across the battlefield when others were hiding in foxholes so that he could tend wounded soldiers or give the dying their last rites. The priest was later awarded a Silver Star for his bravery.

"It was the combination of the influence of Father Basil and the love of the good Lord looking out for me that kept me going," says Prudhomme.

When the Rangers were at a campsite, Father Basil even got Prudhomme on a regular Mass schedule for the first time in his life.

"First thing in the morning, he would get up and ask a few of us to share the Eucharist with him. On some mornings, he would have to kick me in my bunk and ask, 'Are you going to join us?' I always did."

OFF TO ALGERIA

Soon training and preparation were over. It was time for the Rangers to demonstrate their courage on the field of battle. For Prudhomme, engagements with the enemy also provided occasions for God to save his life—and the lives of others—often through seemingly miraculous means.

The First Battalion's initial action was in August 1942 during the Dieppe raid in France. Prudhomme says this engagement, which took place more than two years before D-Day, was the Americans' first ground combat in Europe.

Next the Rangers fought in Algeria, a French colony in North Africa.

"Our ship had anchored off the coast at Gibraltar overnight," recalls Prudhomme. "The next day, we were to land on the beach at Arzew. But my boat landed two miles west of Arzew."

The Rangers were making their way up a ten-foot-tall bluff that rose above the beach. The progress was slow because they were trying to push two-wheel carts carrying mortars and hundreds of pounds of shells. Prudhomme was dispatched to a site at the top of a bluff some three hundred yards ahead and told to guard it. He was given a machine gun, five hundred rounds of ammunition, and this simple order: "If anybody comes down that road, shoot him."

When he heard a sound that resembled footsteps coming his way from the area where enemy soldiers were believed to be hiding, he looked for inspiration in a surprising source: World War I Medal of Honor–recipient Alvin C. York, who confronted a German machine-gun nest, killing twenty Germans and forcing an entire group to surrender.

"I heard a scuffling noise coming up the road. I said, 'Lord, what is that?' And I thought to myself, *What would Sergeant York do?* I decided that Sergeant York would let the enemy soldiers all get by first, then shoot them.

"That's what I decided to do, and as soon as they began to pass me, I heard one of the men stumble and cuss in English. After that, I knew they were American troops who had landed west of us. I was a couple of seconds from machine-gunning those guys down. That was my first miracle, and it still gives me a heart attack to think about it now."

After Algeria, the Rangers went on to Tunisia before landing in Italy. When they invaded Sicily in the summer of 1943, it would be Prudhomme's own life that was miraculously saved. This rocky island off the toe of the Italian boot was the site of the largest amphibious assault of the entire war. Nearly half a million Allied troops were involved in an invasion that was appropriately code-named Husky.

The First Ranger Battalion and the new Third Ranger Battalion were encamped at a spot called Bloody Ridge. Italian pack mules were loaded down with 81-millimeter mortars and were making their way up an exposed stream bed.

Prudhomme describes what happened: "Major Miller wanted some of the men to bring the mortars up the stream bed to his location, so he sent me down there to tell them. As I ran across the stream bed, bursts of machine pistol fire opened up on me.

"I made it to some bushes on the other side, but had to come back. As I made my way, I could hear bullets raining down on me. There were also artillery shells coming in. Two of them landed near me, knocking me down. I got back up and ran to our position, tumbling head over heels as I arrived, crawling the last distance to safety.

"As I caught my breath, I could hear the men moaning. They thought they had just seen me being killed. They came toward me and started looking me over. Then they took off some of my clothes, and there were little bullet holes all through the loose clothing of my uniform, even though I hadn't been hit.

"I felt that I had been blasted out of my senses. I was in such a shook-up condition that a buddy of mine named Maurice Gustavson told me to relax and sit down with him. He decided to smoke his pipe. As soon as he lit that pipe, I looked up, and I could see a German soldier looking down at us from about fifty feet away.

"I can still remember it to this day. He was a typical, movie version of the Aryan-looking German, with blond hair and blue eyes. As he fired at me and Gus, I heard a volley of shots and then a scream. It was one of our own men saying, 'I got the son of a gun.' The German had been killed after firing at me and Gus some eighty-five times.

"Gus and I looked at each other and asked each other if we had been hit. We hadn't, but part of Gus's pipe had been shot off. The pipe stem was still in his mouth."

Such close brushes with death made Prudhomme think about his life and the reasons it may have been spared.

"I have never, never thought that I was just lucky," he asserts. "Up to this very day, I think God has given me another chance to be a better person and to improve myself day after day."

CLOSE CALL AT ANZIO

In January 1944, American and British troops joined together to storm a small port town on the west coast of Italy. The landing at Anzio was designed to outflank the Germans, who were dug in at the Gustav

Line. But nobody had intended the attack to decimate the ranks of the Rangers.

As the battle began, Prudhomme was in a bad way.

"After fighting in Africa and Sicily, I had come down with malaria and jaundice," he says. "I was also struggling with combat fatigue, which was the term they used back then. Now they call it 'delayed stress syndrome.' I was driving an ambulance with Sergeant Ed Wilkerson. Everywhere we went we were fired upon. I think there were thirty-two holes in that ambulance."

Prudhomme and Wilkerson began making their way toward the front lines so they could catch up with their outfit. When they reached the Mussolini Canal, a lieutenant stopped their progress.

"You can't go up there," he said.

That was the day the Third Ranger Battalion and Prudhomme's own First Battalion were routed. Once again, his life had been spared.

BATTLING ENEMIES BACK HOME

By June 1944, Prudhomme had made it back to Natchitoches alive. One of the first things he did was to marry his sweetheart, Lucille. He hadn't written her long love letters in months because he feared he would be dead. Now he couldn't wait to start a family, and before long the couple had two sons.

World War II was over by June 1945, but Prudhomme was still being attacked by some of his own inner demons.

"The war had been rough on me, and when I got out of the service, I was kind of reckless with my life," says Prudhomme, whose main postwar battles were with alcohol and tobacco. "I'm sure the war had something to do with it, but I can't blame it on anybody but myself."

The last twenty years have been different. Prudhomme still struggles with nightmares and bad memories from the war years, and there are days when he is a nervous wreck, but he no longer medicates his nerves with addictive substances.

One might think that the former goldbrick wishes he had never exposed himself to the horrors of war. But this ex-Ranger, who received a Silver Star, a Bronze Star, two Presidential Citations, and Canada's Silver Maple Leaf Wings, says he would do it all over again if he could.

"I did what I was supposed to do," he asserts. "I was a good soldier. I was committed to my country. And I was committed to my fellowman, and I attempted to give my life for some of them more than one time."

His experiences taught Prudhomme that life can be fleeting: "I learned that life is a short thing."

He also realizes that death is not the end of the story, but merely the occasion of the final miracle.

"I attempt to try and stay straight with the Lord," he says. "I don't judge other denominations or other people, but I know the Lord Jesus is my Savior, and I go to bed at night knowing that if I die, I won't get what I deserve because I believe in salvation.

"I don't worry about dying now. All I pray for now is a gentle death. I know that Jesus is my Savior and that God is God. Always was, and always will be."

Ready to serve. Standing at Camp Croft, South Carolina, in 1941, Thomas Prudhomme wasn't sure what his future held. In time he would serve as a member of the elite Rangers unit, which gave him plenty of opportunities to see miracles at close range.

Reunited. During the worst of the fighting, Prudhomme didn't think he would ever get to see his girlfriend, Lucille, again. But the couple were married after his safe return to the U.S. in 1944. The couple are pictured at Fort Smith, Arkansas, with their dog, Spotty.

Faith affirming. Catholic Chaplain Albert Basil (left) encouraged Prudhomme to depend on the resources of his faith. The two men are shown during a 1979 reunion in Philadelphia.

Remembering a Ranger. At a 1995 reunion at Fort Smith, Arkansas, Prudhomme (second from left) and other Rangers remember one of their most famous commanders, Major William Darby of Darby's Rangers.

NINETEEN

JESSE AND NETTIE MILLER

OPEN HEARTS, OPEN HOMES

He was born in a tiny town called Midwest, Wyoming. She was raised on a farm that was even more remote, located between little Montana towns like Manhattan, Amsterdam, and Belgrade that had been settled by hardy Dutch immigrants.

His father died when he was young. So did her mother.

Both had been raised in communities where going to church was as much a part of community life as going to the general store—and often just about as exciting. But during their teen years, both came to the same conclusion: that being a Christian meant more than going to church; it meant having a daily relationship with a living God.

And in time, both sensed a calling to serve God by working as missionaries in Asia. In fact, their faithfulness to that calling made it possible for them to meet each other and led to their ministering together for more than four decades.

Now there is only one. Jesse Miller died in early 2001 after struggling for nearly a decade with the complications of a stroke. Nettie still performs the work of compassion and hospitality that the couple carried out during their many years together. And Cadence International, the organization they founded, still carries out their ministry to military personnel and families near bases throughout the world.

FROM WYOMING TO MANILA

Perhaps it was growing up in rural Wyoming that made young Jesse Miller want to travel. He also had a fascination with photography.

But times were tough in America, and they were tougher still for the Miller family. Jesse's widowed mother worked hard so they could scrape by as best they could.

It seemed to Jesse that the navy would offer him the best chance of realizing his goals and helping his mother financially, so he went to the naval recruiter's office in Casper and volunteered. Everything went OK until the dental exam.

"Too many cavities," said the recruiter. So Jesse walked down the hallway and entered another office. The Army Air Corps wasn't so concerned about dental details, and Jesse enlisted.

As he rode the train out of Cheyenne and headed for training on the West Coast, Jesse thought he was beginning a brief hitch in the army, complete with a free education in photography. After all, that's what the recruiter had promised.

When he finally got out of the service five years, eight months, twenty-three days, eight hours, and twenty-four minutes later after serving as a member of the Twentieth Pursuit Squadron in the Pacific, he didn't know any more about photography than he had when he went in.

He was exceedingly fortunate to be alive after what he had been through, including a period as a prisoner of war in a series of Japanese prisons and slave labor camps.

He had no premonitions of doom as he sailed toward Manila, but he did experience a nagging homesickness. He could have done what many

American servicemen did, carousing in Manila's many bars, clubs, and brothels, but instead he returned to the wellsprings of his faith, which had grown much deeper in the years before he enlisted.

Jesse had been volunteering as the youth leader at his local church. That didn't mean he was particularly religious. He had good organization skills and was willing to work. He helped organize a series of evangelistic services that would be led by a radio preacher from Montana.

When the preacher opened his Bible to Romans 3:23 and preached on the verse that says "all have sinned and fall short of the glory of God," Jesse was stunned. He thought of himself as a good churchgoing kid, not a sinner.

But as he listened to the preacher that night, his heart was transformed.

"If God's word said I was a sinner, it must be true," he wrote in his autobiographical book, *Prisoner of Hope.*

I had never read the Bible for myself. I heard it preached on Sundays, but too often my mind was on things I considered to be more important: photography, Boy Scouting, and stamp collecting.

But that evening the Holy Spirit gave me understanding. I knew I was a sinner and not prepared to meet God. I knew I needed forgiveness and acceptance by my maker.

That night, even before the speaker gave the invitation, I acknowledged that Jesus Christ had taken all my sins and my punishment himself. I believed Christ was my savior! I accepted his forgiveness.

Three years later, Jesse was in the barracks at Clark Field, located sixty miles outside of Manila, when his buddies, trying to console his homesick soul, invited him to join them for a night out on the town.

Jesse went to his locker to start getting dressed, and the Bible his father had given to him before his death fell onto the floor. Jesse decided he would rather read the Bible than join his friends for an evening of mischief.

Even though Jesse felt he was growing closer to God, he still longed for human companionship. That's when he met Cyril and Anna Brooks.

The two missionaries had been in the Philippines for many years working with the local people. But when throngs of American servicemen were stationed in the islands, the couple felt a passion for ministering to them too. One of the ways they did that was by opening their home to soldiers.

For Jesse, the Brookses' house became both his home away from home and his primary source of Christian teaching and discipleship. In particular, Cyril Brooks introduced Jesse to the practice of Scripture memorization, which would remain an important practice to Jesse throughout his life.

"The Brooks family taught me to love and apply the Bible, and extended kind concern, family love, and hospitality to me," he wrote. "I spent more than just the Bible study times with them. At every available opportunity, I found my way to their home."

The love and spiritual growth Jesse Miller experienced there not only helped his faith to mature; they also prepared him for the horrible times that lay ahead.

RETREAT AND SURRENDER

The same day Japanese planes attacked Pearl Harbor, they also hit Clark Field. The camp's barracks, commissary, mess hall, administration building, hospital, and chapel had taken direct hits, and many of the camp's planes were destroyed.

Jesse survived the attack by hiding among the roots of a banyan tree. "I was keenly aware that God was holding me in the hollow of His hand," he said.

Following the attack, Clark Field was evacuated, and the men retreated to the Bataan Peninsula. If the long-promised reinforcements and supplies had arrived, the Americans might have been able to hold out against the Japanese.

But such provisions never came. For three months, tens of thousands of American and Filipino soldiers survived on severely reduced rations, which led to much starvation and disease. For Jesse, though, the difficult months would merely be the beginning of a three-and-a-half-year period of continual hunger and want.

After American forces surrendered to the Japanese, the men were forced to begin the deadly Bataan Death March. Those who were fortunate enough to survive would labor at one of many Japanese prisoner camps.

Jesse was heading into a literal hell on earth, but at the same time, a profound spiritual transformation began to take place in his heart. The reduced rations had ravaged his body with disease and sores, but instead of lashing out in despair and anger, he saw his sufferings as the means by which God was teaching him love and compassion for others.

"I noticed the effects in my own body—swelling, open ulcers, and a major loss of weight. I realized that these ulcers were the same kind of sores I had seen on the Filipino children the day I first arrived in the Philippines. I recalled how repulsed I had been then. I now knew I wasn't a pretty sight either. Suddenly tenderness and sympathy for them overwhelmed me. I was one with them. I found myself wondering how they could be helped."

If suffering is a powerful teacher, Jesse Miller was about to have more than his share of life-changing educational experiences.

BEATEN IN BATAAN

Already weakened by months of reduced rations, as many as eighty thousand American and Filipino soldiers began the Bataan Death March.

The name was an accurate one because as many as fourteen thousand men who began that long journey never finished it. They died of thirst or starvation, they fell unconscious along the road and were left for dead, or they tried to eat something or escape along the way and were killed by the vicious Japanese soldiers who accompanied the miserable convoy.

"Walking dead men, that's what we were," said Jesse, "quite incapable of much thinking and devoid of much feeling."

As the march began, the men were told to lay all their possessions on the ground before them. Jesse had a can of milk in his small pile of goods. Fearing that it would be taken from him, he hurriedly drank it, but was spotted by a guard, who approached and spit on him.

Within Jesse's heart, anger at the guard turned into submission to God.

"My pride flared up in anger," he wrote. "I wanted to strike him. I reasoned that I was bigger than he and given the chance I could whip him, even though I was in a very weakened physical condition.

"But God controlled my actions by bringing into my mind the thought that Christ had been spit upon when He gave His life for me. He took far more rough treatment than I was getting. And He did it for me."

Such humbleness of spirit would help Jesse in the months to come, a time when the humiliations and beatings he endured would increasingly become worse.

At one camp, Jesse worked sixteen or more hours a day mining coal, and like the other prisoners, he was allowed only one day of rest per month. On such days he borrowed a New Testament that one of the men had sneaked into the camp and read what was left of its pages.

This particular New Testament was getting shorter by the day because the prisoners used its thin paper pages to roll cigarettes. The tobacco was collected from the remains of cigarettes the guards had smoked. It bothered Jesse that they would use the Bible in that way, but he had already committed some of the missing passages to memory.

As he was reading the New Testament, Jesse became aware that he was not alone. A guard had seen him reading, and a punishment was forthcoming.

"Beatings weren't new to me," he wrote.

The guards knew just how far to go within an inch of taking life itself.

When the guard began striking me, I wanted to fight back. I weighed 80-90 pounds but I thought I could have struck him hard enough to cause him to stop beating me. Of course I did not vent my anger on him. The bayonet at his side spoke too loudly.

On my fallen body he used his hob-nail boots to do further damage. How long I lay unconscious I do not know. When I awakened I was on my bunk in the barracks. There wasn't a square inch of my body that wasn't torn or bruised.

But perhaps because his soul had been refreshed by reading the New Testament, Jesse once again experienced his suffering as a lesson from God: "My suffering was nothing compared to what people had done to Christ. His back was ripped. He was beaten. He was crucified. Slowly I understood a little better what it cost my Lord to die for me. I began to understand that my suffering was that 'I might know Him and the fellowship of His suffering.'"

Finally, after the prisoners were liberated, Jesse enjoyed his first hot shower in four years, tears of joy mixing with the water that rushed down the drain.

On a transport ship headed for home, he discovered a cafeteria overflowing with food. "Along with the others, I stood in the food line all day for three days," he says. "My weight doubled in about six days."

Welcomed back to Wyoming as a war hero, Jesse was glad to be home. But before long, he would return to Asia as a messenger of God's love.

Called to Teach

While Jesse Miller had been undergoing his torturous imprisonment, Nettie Dyk was going through her own personal transformation on her family's Montana farm. The death of her mother when she was only seven was a major part of the process.

"I was the third of seven children, so my life was a busy one," she says. "Early on I had to learn how to work."

In addition, her entire family had been undergoing a significant spiritual transition.

"My parents had been church members, but when I was quite young, a missionary came to a nearby country schoolhouse and held meetings in the schoolhouse. At that time, my father became a born-again Christian, and that impacted my life. Faith became meaningful to me," she recalls.

"Through the messages I heard in our church, I learned more about what Christianity meant. I began to sense my need for forgiveness and acceptance. One Sunday evening when I was seventeen, I knelt by my bedside and accepted Christ as my Savior. The next morning, I walked out to the barn to tell my father."

After graduating from high school and college, she became a teacher in a one-room schoolhouse outside Laurel, Montana, where she taught seven children, one each in grades one through seven. The next year she taught in a bigger school. It had two rooms.

By 1949 she was a teacher at Green Lake Elementary School in Seattle. While there, she would receive a different call to teach in faraway lands.

"I was rooming with four girls. One of them, Doris Watson, was a secretary who worked for an organization called Far Eastern Gospel Crusade. [The group later changed its name to SEND International.]

"Doris invited me to the organization's weekly prayer meeting. There, we prayed for the needs of missionaries and their ministries. A frequent matter for prayer was that a teacher for missionary children was needed in Japan.

"All the time I had been growing up, my father was very missions minded. We often had missionaries staying in our home. So I knew what missionaries did. At this meeting, I felt that I was being called to answer that prayer request."

Nettie applied for the teaching position and traveled to appear before the ministry's board of directors at their annual meeting in St. Paul, Minnesota. There she met one of the young men who was also applying for a missionary position. His name was Jesse Miller.

"I heard him speak several times that week, and I sensed that he was a man of God," she says. "I felt that what he was saying was not just words, but came from the depth of his being.

"I had covenanted with God that I would not play the field as far as marriage was concerned, and that if God wanted me to marry, He would bring the right person into my life. I would be content with whatever God did. My only request was that He not let me be sorry for myself. And then, very suddenly, I met Jesse."

MISSIONS OR MARRIAGE?

It's not uncommon for single people heading into missions work to fall in love, and sometimes romance replaces the desire for missionary work. The leaders of the ministry wanted to make sure that didn't happen with Jesse and Nettie.

"They sensed there was a connection between Jesse and me," she says. "Because I was needed in Japan and Jesse was needed in the Philippines, the leaders asked us not to see each other.

"They talked to Jesse, and he told them, 'I'm under your authority, and I will not make any attempt to see her.' They told us not to see each other, but they didn't tell us we couldn't write, so we did write some."

Answering the call of God isn't always easy, and Nettie faced her share of struggles en route to her assignment in Asia. On October 21, 1949, she boarded a freighter for Japan. For seventeen of the next twenty-one days, she was seasick. When she landed at the pier in Yokohama, no one came to meet her. The feelings of loneliness were intense.

"I knew that God led me to Japan. I had a sense of calling. I continued to struggle that day, but came to the conclusion God called me; He would care for me, or He would take me home, and it would be OK either way. And I knew that if I died, I would go home to be with the Lord."

Meanwhile, Jesse was on his way to the Philippines. His ship stopped in Japan to unload and take on cargo. During the three days the ship was at Yokohama, Jesse asked Nettie to marry him. She accepted. Then Jesse got back on his ship and headed off for the Philippines while Nettie began her work as a teacher.

On her way back to her compound after seeing him off, she stopped at the post office. There she found three letters from the mission agency saying that the organization would do nothing to stand in the way if God led the two to be married. But Nettie wasn't going to abandon the work God had called her to do in order to get married.

"I really wanted to get my school on its feet before I would marry him," she says. "My special prayer request was that God would provide four new teachers, and He did."

Jesse and Nettie were married in April of 1950. After the unusual romance they had been through, they saw their relationship as a special gift from God.

"Both of us were very committed to what we were called to do," she emphasizes, "but we did not want to put our own ambitions and desires first. In quietness and in confidence, we just trusted the Lord to open the doors, and He did. God worked it all out."

OPEN DOORS IN MANILA

After their marriage in Tokyo and transfer to the Philippines, Nettie taught missionary children while Jesse taught Bible at a Filipino Bible college. Jesse soon became an auxiliary chaplain for the servicemen stationed in and around Manila.

Jim Sheeler, who writes for the *Denver Post,* did an article about the Millers' work in 2001. In the article he quoted a veteran named Tom Hash, who was present for Chaplain Miller's first sermon.

"He was very skinny, left over from his imprisonment," said Hash. "He was quiet and gentle-looking, and as he walked up to the front, the handful of us who were there wondered, 'Who is this guy?'

"Long before he finished his story, we were sitting on the edge of our seats. And that was a typical response. Not long after he began, people would be sitting on the edge of their seats, fascinated."

Jesse regularly invited men who attended the services to come to his house for dinner, fellowship, and further teaching. Soon Jesse and Nettie were following the example of Cyril and Anna Brooks, whose love and hospitality had had such an important impact on Jesse when he was a young and frightened serviceman.

Nettie's childhood experiences helped make this type of ministry a joy. "Practicing hospitality was just a very natural thing for me to do," she says.

Over the next four years the Millers moved three times, getting larger houses to accommodate the growing numbers of soldiers, sailors, and marines who ate and visited with them.

In 1954 the couple formalized their ministry, creating an organization called the Overseas Christian Servicemen's Centers, which recruited workers to minister to military personnel all over the world. And in 1957, they moved to Denver, initially operating the ministry out of the basement of their house. The organization's name was later changed to Cadence International.

A MINISTRY CONTINUES

Today Cadence International carries on the ministry of hospitality begun by Jesse and Nettie Miller in their home in the Philippines.

Cadence International is a nondenominational, evangelical mission working in over forty locations worldwide, says John Miller, Jesse and Nettie s youngest son, who works for Cadence, and our mission is sharing the gospel and our lives with the military community.

Currently nearly 240 trained staff and volunteers work near military bases in Germany, Italy, Spain, the Philippines, Korea, Japan, and the U.S. In recent years the ministry has also launched programs in Russia and the former countries of the Soviet Union. These programs are run by former Russian military personnel.

There are nearly four million members of the U.S. military community, including men, women, and teens, says John Miller.

The military subculture is one of the largest and most responsive to the gospel today, and many of today s missionaries were first exposed to other people groups while in the military.

For information on Cadence International write to P.O. Box 1268, Englewood, CO 80150; phone 1-303-762-1400; or visit the organization s Web site (www.cadence.org).

For information on Jesse Miller s book, *Prisoner of Hope,* visit the www.prisonerofhope.info Web site.

Nettie remains an advocate for the ministry of hospitality. "Paul's letter to the Romans tells Christians to show hospitality, especially to the saints," she says. "I believe it's one of the Christian virtues."

A Lasting Legacy

Jesse suffered a debilitating stroke in 1992. Unable to speak or write, he was initially frustrated with his condition. But then he began to treat his condition the same way he had treated his time in the prison camp: as an opportunity to learn more about God's grace.

"He was a gentle person," says Nettie. "He knew what it was to suffer, and he took suffering far better than I did."

The work to which the Millers dedicated their lives hasn't stopped. Instead, it is carried on by more than two hundred Cadence International workers.

"The Lord has certainly multiplied it," she notes. "It's amazing how many homes have been opened."

And Nettie still opens up her home to others on a regular basis. "I host a special prayer meeting here at the house every month for those who served in Cadence," she says. "It's the old-timers.

"The week before we get together, I contact all our missionaries and ask them what their immediate prayer requests are. Then I type these on a computer and print them out so everyone has a copy. We meet on a Saturday morning. I fix breakfast, we all sit at table, and we pray."

Remembering Christ. Miller was regularly beaten and abused, but instead of turning against his guards, he reflected on how Christ had endured much more suffering out of love for a fallen humanity.

Nettie and Jesse. Both Jesse Miller and Nettie Dyk had felt a calling to serve God through missionary service. For four decades they served together.

Dinnertime! As a soldier, Jesse Miller had appreciated the Christian hospitality that was shown to him while he was a young soldier in the Philippines. Later he and Nettie showed similar hospitality to other servicemen, giving birth to the Overseas Christian Servicemen's Centers, now known as Cadence International. Nettie is shown at left with the couple's oldest son, Jim. Jesse isn't shown; he's taking the picture.

Seeing the world. Jesse Miller thought his time in the Army Air Corps would enable him to see the world and learn about photography. Instead, he was an aircraft mechanic who learned a deeper love for Christ.

TWENTY

HOWARD HEATON

BEHIND THE SILENCE OF THE SILENT GENERATION

The people who participated in World War II used to be called the silent generation. That's because many of the men and women left farms and towns while they were still teenagers and were thrust into one of the most horrifying and destructive wars the world has ever seen.

Physically the youngsters were pushed to the breaking point and beyond, while psychologically they were traumatized by atrocity and brutality on such an unprecedented scale that their memories remain, for many, unspeakable.

Those among them who were fortunate enough to come back home wanted to get on with their lives and put the terrible scenes of death and destruction behind them. As a result, many veterans never told their friends, their children, or even their spouses about their war experiences.

A character in the 1943 movie *Guadalcanal Diary* spoke for many of these quiet veterans when he said, "I'm no hero. I'm just a guy. I come out here because somebody had to come. I don't want medals. I just want to get this over with and go back home. I'm just like everybody else, and I'm telling you, I don't like it."

But many members of the silent generation began to open up in 1998. In that year two projects that had been long in the works emerged and struck a resounding chord with millions of Americans of all ages.

In movie theaters Steven Spielberg's Oscar-winning *Saving Private Ryan* harnessed the evocative power of film to portray the awful carnage of the D-Day invasion and the extravagant kindness shown to one soldier whose brothers had died fighting.

And in bookstores, NBC News anchor Tom Brokaw's *The Greatest Generation* flew off the shelves, inspiring two Brokaw sequels and launching a flood of successful World War II books.

Since then, many veterans have begun excavating memories and telling stories that had been buried for six decades.

People listened, in part because veterans were dying at an alarming rate, taking their untold stories to their graves with them. In addition many of the books and movies came out long after the Gulf War of the early 1990s had ended and before Arab terrorists attacked the World Trade Center and the Pentagon.

Having no war of their own, baby boomers latched on to World War II with gusto. In fact, there has been such a deluge of stories that *New York Times* writer Maureen Dowd cried foul.

"There is a blitzkrieg of World War II reunions, oral histories, Web sites, panels, TV specials," she wrote. The silent generation had become the greatest generation, which had finally become "the gabbiest generation."

Howard Heaton, though, is one of many, many people who have not joined the gabfest. Like many veterans, Heaton remains reticent about what he did in the war and its impact on him. Some of the things he experienced were so devastating that his mind shut down. As a result, he doesn't recall what happened to him much of the time.

"The fact is, I don't have a lot of action stories," says Heaton, who probably wouldn't have considered being a part of this book if his daughter hadn't twisted his arm.

"I have very few memories. I can only assume that this was my reaction to the circumstances I went through. I have not talked to anyone about the war. And I can't even remember names of areas where I was stationed. These names don't mean a thing to me."

Heaton's interview for this book took longer than any of the others, but produced the fewest words. His memories came out in bits and bursts rather than in a strong, steady stream. And many of these memories show why so many World War II veterans prefer to keep their memories to themselves.

FARMING AND FAITH

Howard Heaton was born November 23, 1924, on a farm near Elberon, Iowa. He was delivered by his father, Donald, who, when he wasn't supervising the birth of babies, was raising hogs and dairy cattle and harvesting corn, oats, and soybeans.

Heaton's mother, Faye, did her best to keep the family together during the dark days of the Great Depression, but there were times when the pressure wore her down.

"I remember a number of times my mother going into the basement stairway and crying because she didn't know exactly how she was going to feed me, my younger sister, her husband, and herself," Heaton says.

Christianity was a fundamental part of life in rural Iowa and in Heaton's family. Faith helped them survive the tough times. But as he looked around, Heaton saw that even in a tiny place like Elberon, some people seemed to use religiosity as a means to improve their social standing rather than draw them closer to God.

"Going to church was just part of our life at that time," he says. "It was part of the social establishment, and it was one of the few opportunities people had to meet their neighbors. On Saturday night you would go to a band concert if there was one in town, and on Sunday you dressed up and you went to church."

But in Heaton's home, the commitment to Christ was solid, and faith was vibrant.

"With my parents it went much deeper," he emphasizes. "They lived it. They were not religious fanatics; they were tolerant people.

"We gave thanks for every meal. When I was younger, we prayed before I went to bed. We read the Bible together in the evenings, and we prayed together."

In addition to Christian teaching, Heaton absorbed a set of social values as he grew up: "We believed in hard work, respect for other people, and the need to look out for your fellowman."

This last value was something Heaton's mother put in practice, being gone from the family for long periods of time to care for an ailing sister.

But looking out for your fellowman meant more than caring for family members. It also meant standing up for your country.

"There was a deep respect for our democratic way of life, and for preserving that way of life," he says.

"There was a type of life we had lived, and we wanted this to continue. So when this fellow named Hitler showed up attempting to take over Europe, the threat was there. You had to respond."

FROM IOWA TO NORMANDY

When Japan attacked Pearl Harbor, Heaton was still in high school. He planned to enlist as soon as he graduated in 1943, but he had committed to helping a neighbor with his farming that fall, so he left Iowa in November of that year.

After training, Heaton was made a private in the Seventeenth Airborne Division assigned to the 194th Glider Battalion. He was shipped out to England, the staging area for the gigantic D-Day invasion of northern France.

Like many of the fighting men, Heaton wasn't told about the entire scope of the operation, but was instructed in his own duties and responsibilities. He and other members of the airborne troops would fly over the Channel into France.

"To what degree we were in any real danger, we didn't know," he recalls. "All we could imagine was that we were a part of something very dramatic."

But soon drama turned into destruction. As the airborne fighters landed in France, men Heaton had trained with fell dead to his right and his left. Almost immediately his mind worked overtime to compensate for the shock he experienced on a moment-by-moment basis.

"I don't believe I ever really feared dying," he says. "I was just kind of numb to any real feeling. You would see someone get hit by shrapnel, and it would take off their arm. Of course, you're concerned for that person, but I wouldn't say I developed a fear for my own life. I guess the way my mind handled it was to keep me from being afraid."

Heaton knew he didn't want to go through what had happened to a cousin of his.

"The minute he walked off the troop ship in England, he lost it," he says. "They sent him back."

Rather than giving in to despair, Heaton placed his faith in God.

"From the minute I flew into France, I always figured the good Lord had His hand in everything and would take care of me."

TEDIUM AND TRAVEL

After successfully landing at Normandy's beaches in June 1944, Allied forces penetrated deeper into the French countryside, fighting retreating German troops at every step of the way.

COMBAT CASUALTIES: DID WORLD WAR II VETS SUFFER FROM POST-TRAUMATIC STRESS DISORDER?

The millions of American servicemen who survived in World War II were welcomed home as victorious heroes. Then they quietly went about the business of normal life. Among other things, their efforts fueled a boom in postwar births, economic growth, and missionary activity.

Decades later, though, veterans of the war in Vietnam came home to a completely different world. America had failed to win the conflict in Asia, and back at home, many Americans criticized returning soldiers for having fought in such a controversial and unpopular war.

In addition, veterans returning from Vietnam complained about the psychological suffering they had endured. In time psychiatrists developed a term to describe their suffering: *post-traumatic stress disorder.*

The *Diagnostic and Statistical Manual of Mental Disorders,* a reference book published by the American Psychiatric Association, reports that the disorder is brought about by a psychologically distressing event that is outside the range of usual human experience.

All people encounter difficulties in life, and stressful events like bereavement, chronic illness, business setbacks, and marital discord routinely add to people s discomfort. But the kinds of events that are said to cause post-traumatic stress disorder go beyond these fairly common tragedies. Among the events that can cause the disorder are those that are experienced with intense fear, terror, and helplessness, and involve either a serious threat to one s life or physical integrity or seeing another person who is being . . . seriously injured or killed.

Trauma is something that can be experienced alone (rape or assault) or in groups (an airplane crash), and causes can be natural in origin (tornadoes and hurricanes) or the efforts of other human beings (terrorist acts). But psychiatrists believe that the disorder is apparently more severe and longer lasting when the stressor is of human design.

People suffering from post-traumatic stress disorder reexperience their trauma in a variety of ways, both when awake and when dreaming. And in trying to cope with the disorder, sufferers try to avoid troubling stimuli. In doing so, many experience psychic numbing or emotional anesthesia as well as depression and anxiety.

Many of these symptoms sound precisely like the things that many members of World War II s silent generation experienced. If that is the case, why didn t psychiatrists determine that these fighting men had experienced post-traumatic stress disorder like the men who fought in Vietnam?

The answer is largely one of history. Although psychology has been around in various forms for thousands of years, it was only in the eighteenth and nineteenth centuries that it ceased to be seen as a field of study within philosophy and gradually became more of a science. The work of Sigmund Freud, a pioneer in the field of psychoanalysis, helped fuel this transformation in the late 1800s. When soldiers served in World War II, psychology was still a specialty practice.

Some American forces did engage in psychological warfare, which usually consisted of propaganda efforts designed to convince enemy fighters that their cause was unjust and hopeless. But when it came to psychological healing, few people suggested that returning American soldiers could benefit from such services, and fewer still knew how to deliver them.

By the 1960s, though, psychological concepts like *personality disorders* and *self-esteem* were household terms. As a result, Vietnam veterans complaints about their wartime suffering were treated as psychiatric problems.

Most veterans of World War II did not benefit from such diagnoses and care, but it is obvious from listening to many of their stories that they suffered just as much as later fighting men did.

One of the biggest showdowns of the war would be the Battle of the Bulge, much of which centered on the strategically important Belgian town of Bastogne in the rough winter of 1944. Heaton was part of the massive American effort making preparations for this decisive showdown.

"At one point I was driving a truck twenty-four hours a day for five straight days moving supplies, ammunition, and food to Bastogne," he recalls. "During that time I learned I could sleep standing up. If there were a few minutes when someone was loading or unloading the truck, I would lean up against it and sleep for a few minutes."

Although Heaton never tried sleeping while driving, others apparently did.

"I remember being part of a big convoy heading back from Bastogne to pick up more supplies. It was a long, mostly one-lane road. As I drove through the night, my job was to follow the truck directly ahead of me.

"For a while, I lost him. Then as daybreak was coming on, I noticed that the truck didn't have a trailer on it. When we started out, he did have a trailer. He had gone off the road at night and lost his trailer."

During the ensuing weeks and months, the tedium of nonstop work was getting to Heaton. One time when he had a brief chance to sleep lying down, he threw his blanket into what he thought was a foxhole. Hours later he awoke to an overpowering stench. He lay down in a latrine, but he was so tired, he hadn't even noticed.

Heaton was also involved in his share of shocking encounters with the enemy, but he isn't sure where they happened or what the outcomes were.

"I remember heavy enemy shelling as we were coming into Bastogne," he says, "but there's an awful lot I don't remember.

"I do remember one particular sunny day, which was unusual in the foggy winter. You could hear the shells coming in, and the men running and hiding in cellars of houses and anywhere else they could find cover. Some of us saw a manure pile and were thinking about jumping in. Then one of the shells hit the manure pile. There was no place to go."

As for minor skirmishes with enemy soldiers, they were common.

"I had a rifle, and I shot it, but to say I killed somebody, I couldn't say. I just don't know."

A Catalog of Horrors and Close Calls

Heaton doesn't remember precisely where he was and exactly what he did during weeks of the cruel winter of 1944–45. But he does recall a catalog of wartime horrors that slip out of his memory like fragments of a nightmare.

"One thing I remember was that as winter came on there, it was a very severe winter with a lot of snow. The way we lost a lot of our guys was that they froze to death.

"I can still see truckloads of bodies, frozen in grotesque shapes, as they were transported from the front. Some lay as if they were in position to fire at the enemy. Some were frozen on one knee like toy soldiers. These were the positions they were in when they picked them up."

Heaton and other members of the airborne troops were flying across the Rhine River in twelve-man gliders.

"Many of the gliders were coming under heavy fire and didn't make it across. In another case one of the gliders crashed after takeoff because one of its wings fell off.

"Our glider made it across OK to the friendly side of the Rhine. But after we landed, we inspected our glider and saw that a bolt was about to fall off the bracing that was holding on one of our wings. That was another close call."

Other horrible memories come back to haunt Heaton.

"We would go into a house looking for enemy soldiers, and there would be something there that on first reaction I thought were dolls lying there on the floor. Instead, it was tiny children lying dead, bloated up, and blue.

"Some older children were fighting for the Germans, who were rapidly running out of manpower. Some of these young soldiers were children who looked like they were between twelve and sixteen years of age. While they were taught well, they lacked any real experience with warfare."

After fighting in Bastogne, Heaton found himself in Dresden, which had been pounded by air bombardments, killing as many as 100,000 soldiers, civilians, and refugees.

"The town was destroyed," he says. "But after things died down, I realized that I had not taken my shoes off for a month. When I did, my toes and heels were black."

But Heaton was more fortunate than many. And death seemed to lurk everywhere, even under the mounds of white snow.

"I remember standing at the side of a roadway as a column of tanks passed by. As the tanks passed over the snow, you could see the intestines of dead soldiers rise up out of snow. Even now, it seems a little odd to me that memories like this are so much clearer and much more precise than details about battles and places where I was.

"I can only assume that this was my reaction to the circumstances I was experiencing. And frankly I have not talked to anyone about a lot of these things."

Throughout the months of agony, Heaton prayed to God for protection and deliverance.

"I would kind of turn everything over to the good Lord, and I still do," he says. "Back then, much of it was foxhole prayers, pleading with God and then giving thanks for every time I came out of something alive and OK.

"Due to a lot of things, I am convinced that the only reason I survived was because God had a plan for me. I'm not sure exactly what that plan was. Maybe it was just to survive and lead a normal life.

"But whatever it was, it had to be something beyond comprehension when I had so many friends blown away in my outfit, sometimes just a few feet from you. What else can explain the fact that they're gone and you're still there?"

BACK TO IOWA

Like many other American fighting men, Heaton was understandably relieved when World War II was over and he could return home.

Heaton went back to Iowa as quickly as he could and with as little fanfare as possible.

"There was a chance for some of us to go to New York and walk down Fifth Avenue in a big parade," says Heaton. "But that was no big deal. I had walked across Europe. There was no need to walk down Fifth Avenue."

Heaton was more interested in reuniting with Darlene, whom he had married hurriedly before he left for Europe.

"I loved the girl, and that was good enough for me," says Heaton, who admits he had second thoughts about whether it was best to wed before he went away.

"I wanted her to be a part of my life. It was really unfair to both parties, but neither of us was sorry for getting married."

But Darlene says the man who came back from World War II wasn't the same man who left some two years earlier.

"He was more nervous than he had ever been before," she recalls. "And I learned that I didn't walk up behind him or startle him."

Heaton knows the war changed him forever, but he prefers thinking about the positive changes it brought about in his life rather than dwelling on the negative.

"Serving gave me more maturity," he says. "And I did what I was supposed to do. I wouldn't have done it any other way."

Based in Berlin. Howard Heaton is shown in his apartment in Berlin. He taught motor mechanics to Allied troops while stationed there. Nearby, results of the Allied bombing campaign were evident throughout the city.

Comrades in arms. Howard Heaton (right) and a fellow serviceman pose for the camera while serving in Europe.

TWENTY-ONE

DIETRICH BONHOEFFER

WORLDLY CHRISTIAN

In late 1999, scholars, journalists, and pundits were working overtime to devise various "best of" lists that ranked the most important of the twentieth century's many achievements. Arguments erupted when rival film critics disagreed over one another's conflicting claims that a particular movie was one of the best films of the century. Meanwhile, scientists debated one another to determine which of the century's numerous technological developments would be hailed as most significant.

But there was one thing list makers agreed on. When it was time to draw up lists of the century's top religious books, Dietrich Bonhoeffer's *The Cost of Discipleship* repeatedly made the top ten.

Bonhoeffer was a pastor, a theologian, a teacher, and a writer, but part of what makes his work have such a continuing relevance is that he was engaged in a passionate struggle to understand the practical implications of his deep Christian faith at a time when the world seemed to be getting much more complex and morally ambiguous.

"It is becoming clearer every day that the most urgent problem besetting our Church is this: How can we live the Christian life in the modern world?" he wrote in *The Cost of Discipleship*, a thoughtful and inspiring book that is so much more.

Bonhoeffer wrestled with many profound questions, but one he returned to time and time again was how to live a life of radical devotion to Christ without settling instead for "pious humbug."

He was certainly intellectual enough to engage in theological hairsplitting, but he had a pastor's heart and repeatedly engaged in something he called a "turning away from the phraseological to the real."

As he thought more about the fundamentals of the Christian faith, he reflected on the importance of the Incarnation. He concluded that the act of God becoming a man to reach the human race was an important model for Christians to follow. As he wrote in *The Cost of Discipleship*: "The Incarnation is the ultimate reason why the service of God cannot be divorced from the service of man."

Bonhoeffer believed the world was awash in something he called "cheap grace," which stripped Christianity of its true power to transform people's lives and the societies in which they live. He challenged readers to go deeper. Or as he said in one of his most memorable lines, "When Christ calls a man, He bids him come and die."

Those words would be eerily prophetic. When confronted with the evils of a totalitarian Nazi regime that came to power in his native Germany, Bonhoeffer became a member of the resistance, ultimately paying for his rebellion with the cost of his life.

He was not the only German Christian to suffer such a fate, but he was clearly in the minority. Today his legacy of commitment and sacrifice continues to illumine minds and warm hearts around the world.

FAITH OF HIS FATHERS

Dietrich Bonhoeffer was born on February 4, 1906. His family was part of a German Christian tradition that traced its roots back nearly four centuries to the time of Protestant Reformer Martin Luther, but his father was also a modern man, becoming the first person to occupy a chair of psychiatry at a German university.

The family was loving, and Bonhoeffer would remain close to his parents, his three brothers, and his four sisters throughout his life.

The family was also devout, but religious devotion was combined with a love for nature, music, art, and literature. Bonhoeffer decided by the age of fourteen that he would be a theologian, and he began teaching at Berlin University in 1929 when he was only twenty-three years old.

World War I had not only devastated much of Europe and killed off millions of its young people, but the Great War also infused European philosophy and theology with a deep strain of pessimism about humanity and society. Theologians like Karl Barth, a founder of neoorthodoxy, responded to these concerns by returning to the Bible for clues it might hold to the dilemmas of modern life.

In 1930, Bonhoeffer traveled to the United States to study at Union Theological Seminary in New York, where he made two important discoveries. First, his friendship with Reinhold and H. Richard Niebuhr, two of the nation's leading theologians, exposed him to intellectual trends on this side of the Atlantic. And second, he met some of the pioneers of the civil rights movement. The lessons he learned from African-American religious thinkers would play a crucial role in his later activities in the German resistance.

Barth, the Niebuhrs, and the civil rights leaders were inspirations to Bonhoeffer, who read the Bible with new eyes before he wrote his first two books, *Creation and Fall* and *Christ the Center*, which were based on his Berlin University lectures.

Then in 1933, Adolf Hitler was named Germany's chancellor, and Nazism quickly became more popular throughout the country. Bonhoeffer saw the Nazi ideology as incompatible with Christianity on many issues, including its approach toward the Jews, and he also grew concerned about the German people's growing infatuation with Hitler, a totalitarian dictator who promised to deliver them from their many trials and tribulations.

During a 1933 broadcast on Berlin radio, Bonhoeffer voiced his concerns, chastising his countrymen for embracing a "leader" who was bound to become a "misleader." Censors cut off the broadcast before it was finished, but Bonhoeffer would continue to have differences with the Third Reich and would continue to speak publicly about those differences, no matter what the cost.

PATRIOTISM VS. PIETY

As long as people have lived in nations, national pride and a sense of divine blessing have been an important part of civic life. There's nothing inherently wrong with combining patriotism and piety, but Dietrich Bonhoeffer could foresee that the growth of Nazism would force Christians to evaluate whether their first allegiance was to their heavenly Father or the German fatherland.

In the 1930s many pastors pledged their allegiance to the German Christian Church, which the Nazis largely controlled. But others, like Martin Niemoeller, helped found a Confessing Church movement that remained independent of government control. Karl Barth wrote the movement's defining document, the *Barmen Declaration,* which challenged German churches to remain faithful to the truths of the gospel and reject the temptations of nationalist religion and totalitarianism.

Following his 1933 radio broadcast, Bonhoeffer would have additional run-ins with the Nazis, who prohibited him from teaching or speaking in public. In time he would join the Confessing Church movement, and by 1935 he was the head of the movement's underground German seminary.

Bonhoeffer traveled to the United States in 1939 for a lecture tour,

A WEALTH OF
BONHOEFFER RESOURCES

Today Christians around the world still read Bonhoeffer s *The Cost of Discipleship, Life Together,* and *Letters and Papers from Prison.*

Recent years have also seen an outpouring of award-winning materials that document the courage and commitment of this unique modern martyr: Bonhoeffer: The Cost of Freedom is a two-hour program produced for Focus on the Family s Radio Theater (Tyndale, 1997); *Bonhoeffer: Agent of Grace* and *Hanged on a Twisted Cross* are acclaimed video presentations available from Vision Video (call 1-800-523-0226; or visit www.visionvideo.com); and *Christian History* magazine devoted an entire issue to Bonhoeffer (issue 32, vol. 10, no. 4).

for by that time his writings and his resistance had made him an international celebrity. While in the U.S. he received many offers to stay there instead of returning to the growing confusion in his native land. But Bonhoeffer felt a strong calling to return.

In a letter to Reinhold Niebuhr, Bonhoeffer spelled out his reasoning: "I shall have no right to participate in the reconstruction of Christian life in Germany after the war if I do not share in the trials of this time with my people."

He returned to Germany, and as the Third Reich became increasingly powerful, Bonhoeffer became a member of the underground resistance movement. Along with people like his brother-in-law Hans von Dohnanyi, Bonhoeffer actively worked to overthrow the Nazi government and assist its foreign enemies.

That was a fateful step for a man who had once believed the way to combat evil was through passive resistance. As we will see, it would be a fateful decision. But as he wrote in *The Cost of Discipleship*, one's commitment to God had to override obligations to one's country: "Jesus knows all about . . . the representatives and preachers of the national religion, who enjoy greatness and renown, whose feet are firmly planted on the earth, who are deeply rooted in the culture and piety of the people and moulded by the spirit of the age."

Meanwhile, other preachers could see the evil at the heart of the Nazi regime: "They see that for all the jollity on board, the ship is beginning to sink."

LIFE IN COMMUNITY

Bonhoeffer agreed to lead the Confessing Church movement's underground seminary in 1935. Within two years, the school had been shut down by the Gestapo, but his time at the seminary was one of the most productive periods of his life.

Throughout that period he lived with about two dozen students in a community setting that, in some ways, resembled a Protestant monastery. Out of that experience and his formal lectures would come his 1938 book, *Life Together: A Discussion of Christian Fellowship*.

"It is easily forgotten that the fellowship of Christian brethren is a gift of grace," he wrote, "a gift of the Kingdom of God that any day may be taken from us."

Life in community could be difficult, especially when people came into the experience with unrealistic expectations. Yet Bonhoeffer became convinced that fellowship could help followers of Christ learn to become more godly and develop a heart for serving their fellow believers.

"The first service that one owes to others in the fellowship consists in listening to them," he wrote. "Many people are looking for an ear that will listen. They do not find it among Christians, because these Christians are talking where they should be listening. But he who can no longer listen to his brother will soon be no longer listening to God either."

While at the seminary, Bonhoeffer would also deliver the lectures that would be published as *The Cost of Discipleship*. Much of the book is insightful and quotable, but one of the more powerful passages is Bonhoeffer's discussion of the differences between true discipleship and something he called "cheap grace":

Cheap grace is the deadly enemy of our Church. We are fighting today for costly grace.

Cheap grace means grace sold on the market like cheapjacks' wares. The sacraments, the forgiveness of sin, and the consolations of religion are thrown away at cut prices. Grace is presented as the Church's inexhaustible treasury, from which she showers blessings with generous hands, without asking questions or fixing limits. Grace without price; grace without cost! The essence of grace, we suppose, is that the account has been paid in advance; and, because it has been paid, everything can be had for nothing. Since the cost was infinite, the possibilities of using and spending it are infinite. What would grace be if it were not cheap?

Cheap grace means grace as a doctrine, a principle, a system. It means forgiveness of sins proclaimed as a general truth, the love of God taught as the Christian "conception" of God. An intellectual assent to that idea is held to be of itself sufficient to secure remission of sins. The Church which holds the correct doctrine of grace has, it is supposed, ipso facto a part in that grace. In such a Church the world finds a cheap covering for its sins; no contrition is required, still less any real desire to be delivered from sin. Cheap grace therefore amounts to a denial of the living Word of God, in fact, a denial of the Incarnation of the Word of God.

Cheap grace is the preaching of forgiveness without requiring repentance, baptism without Church discipline, Communion without confession, absolution without personal confession. Cheap grace is grace without discipleship, grace without the cross, grace without Jesus Christ, living and incarnate.

Costly grace is the treasure hidden in the field; for the sake of it a man will gladly go and sell all that he has. It is the pearl of great price to buy which the merchant will sell all his goods. It is the kingly rule of Christ, for whose sake a man will pluck out the eye which causes him to stumble, it is the call of Jesus Christ at which the disciple leaves his nets and follows him.

Costly grace is the gospel which must be sought again and again, the gift which must be asked for, the door at which a man must knock.

Such grace is costly because it calls us to follow, and it is grace because it calls us to follow Jesus Christ. It is costly because it costs a man his life, and it is grace because it gives a man the only true life. It is costly because it condemns sin, and grace because it justifies the sinner. Above all, it is costly because it cost God the life of his Son: "ye were bought at a price," and what has cost God much cannot be cheap for us. Above all, it is grace because God did not reckon his Son too dear a price to pay for our life, but delivered him up for us. Costly grace is the Incarnation of God.

Costly grace is the sanctuary of God; it has to be protected from the world, and not thrown to the dogs. It is therefore the living word, the Word of God, which he speaks as it pleases him. Costly grace confronts us as a gracious call to follow Jesus, it comes as a word of forgiveness to the broken spirit and the contrite heart. Grace is costly because it compels a man to submit to the yoke of Christ and follow him; it is grace because Jesus says: "My yoke is easy and my burden is light." (From the anthology *The Martyred Christian*, ed. Joan Winmill Brown)

Clearly Bonhoeffer believed in speaking the truth, but he also believed in living out his faith. As he became more and more convinced that the Third Reich was an evil regime, he stepped up his resistance efforts, serving for a time as a double agent. Such activities would lead to his imprisonment and death.

A PRIVATE PATMOS

Even in the worst of times, life goes on. In January 1943, Dietrich Bonhoeffer became engaged to be married. But the marriage would never happen. On April 5, 1943, Bonhoeffer, his brother-in-law Hans von Dohnanyi, and others who had plotted against the Nazis were arrested.

Bonhoeffer was eventually taken to Tegel Prison in Berlin. The atmosphere was horrible. Guards were abusive, and some prisoners screamed throughout the days and nights. To make matters worse, as Allied forces drew closer to Berlin, prisoners were repeatedly subjected to bombing attacks, which left their nerves frazzled and the windows of their cells broken.

Bonhoeffer made the best of his time by praying, reading the Bible, and singing hymns to himself. In time his guard befriended him, giving him paper and pens, and even delivering his letters and writings to friends outside the prison. "I am sure you will understand," he wrote in one letter, "that considering things takes up a large part of my life here."

After his death, much of what Bonhoeffer wrote would be published in the book *Letters and Papers from Prison,* which, like *The Cost of Discipleship,* was widely hailed as one of the best religious books of the twentieth century.

Easter and Christmastime were particularly difficult because Bonhoeffer experienced a strong desire to worship with other believers. "I longed to go to church," he wrote in June 1943, "but instead I did as John did on the island of Patmos, and had such a splendid service of my own that I did not feel lonely at all."

One of the most surprising things about Bonhoeffer's prison writings

A DIETRICH BONHOEFFER TIME LINE

1906 Born in Breslau, Germany

1923 Begins theological studies at Tubingen University

1924 Begins studies at Berlin University

1928 Serves as assistant pastor in Barcelona, Spain

1929 Begins assistant teaching at Berlin University

1930 Begins year of study at Union Theological Seminary in New York

1931 Appointed lecturer in theology at Berlin University

1933 Opposes the Aryan Clause excluding Jews from the ministry in the German church

1934 Confessing Church adopts *Barmen Declaration*

1935 Heads Confessing Church movement s underground seminary

1936 Terminated at Berlin University because he s an enemy of state

1937 *The Cost of Discipleship* published

1938 *Life Together* published; Bonhoeffer forbidden to live or work in Berlin

1939 Travels to United States for lecture tour in June

1939 Returns to Germany in July to suffer with his people

1939 Becomes a double agent for the German military intelligence in August

1943 Engaged to Maria von Wedemeyer in January

1943 Arrested and put in Tegel Prison in April

1943 Begins writing in July the letters and memoirs that will be published in 1944 as *Letters and Papers from Prison*

1945 Moved to Buchenwald concentration camp in February

1945 On April 8 Hitler gives order to annihilate the Canaris resistance group, of which Bonhoeffer is a coconspirator

1945 Bonhoeffer hanged in Flossenburg concentration camp on April 9

is the sense of hopefulness, calmness, and contentedness that he found in his dismal circumstances.

"I believe that God can and will bring good out of evil, even out of the greatest evil," he wrote. "Much as I long to be out of here, I don't believe a single day has been wasted. What will come out of my time here it is still too early to say, but something will come of it."

Like all believers, Bonhoeffer lived in the tension between the sufferings and trials of the present moment and the deep hope for a better day: "There remains for us only the very narrow way, often extremely difficult to find, of living every day as if it were our last, and yet living in faith and responsibility as though there were to be a great future."

Bonhoeffer repeatedly stated that he had no regrets about his actions that led to his imprisonment. Rather, he found contentment in his circumstances, as imperfect as they were: "I am traveling with gratitude and cheerfulness along the road where I am being led."

Bonhoeffer continued to hope that he would be released. He grew more pessimistic, though, after a July 1944 effort to assassinate Hitler failed, and the Third Reich clamped down even more on its opponents.

Nevertheless, he remained committed to living out his faith, as he wrote on July 21, 1944, the day after the failed assassination attempt:

> During the past year or so I have come to know and understand more and more the profound this-worldliness of Christianity . . . I don't mean the shallow and banal this-worldliness of the enlightened, the busy, the comfortable, or the lascivious, but the profound this-worldliness, characterized by discipline and the constant knowledge of death and resurrection.
>
> It is only by living completely in this world that one learns to have faith.
>
> By this-worldliness I mean living unreservedly in life's duties, problems, successes and failures, experiences and perplexities. In doing so we throw ourselves completely into the arms of God, taking seriously, not our own sufferings, but those of God in the world—watching with Christ in Gethsemane.
>
> So I am grateful for the past and present, and content with them.
>
> May God in his mercy lead us through these times; but above all may he lead us to himself.

THE LAST DAYS

In February 1945 an Allied bomb destroyed the Tegel Prison, and Bonhoeffer was taken to the Buchenwald concentration camp. From there he was taken to a series of prisons and camps, and all contact with the outside world was severed.

By the time he arrived at the Flossenburg camp, the Gestapo had learned of yet another effort to kill Hitler. As a result, Bonhoeffer and other prisoners who had actively opposed Hitler were condemned to be executed in the waning days of the Nazi regime.

On Sunday, April 8, 1945, Bonhoeffer was leading a church service at Flossenburg. One of the other believers who was present at the service records what happened next: "He had hardly finished his last prayer when the door opened and two evil-looking men in civilian clothes came in and said, 'Prisoner B, get ready to come with us.' Those words, 'come with us'—for all prisoners they had come to mean one thing only—the scaffold."

The next day, Bonhoeffer was executed. No one knows where he was buried. Three days later, Allied troops liberated the Flossenburg camp and freed those who were still alive.

Payne Best, an English officer who had been at the prison with Bonhoeffer, later recorded his memories of the man. "Bonhoeffer was all humility and sweetness," he wrote. "He always seemed to me to diffuse an atmosphere of happiness, of joy in every smallest event in life, and of deep gratitude for the mere fact that he was alive. He was one of the very few men I have ever met to whom God was real and close."

More than half a century later, people are still praising the German pastor who stood up to the Nazis. Two scholars gave their assessments in a special issue of *Christian History* magazine dedicated to his legacy.

Scholar John D. Godsey wrote, "Despite his sometimes jarring, controversial statements, Bonhoeffer has elicited a positive response from all types of Christians—liberals and conservatives—and from non-Christians as well. All these people find in Bonhoeffer's life and thought a challenging faith that is worth living for, and dying for."

And in an article titled "Radical Resistance," historian Richard V. Pierard remarked, "Dietrich Bonhoeffer's life and death left a clear legacy for subsequent generations of Christians. From his shining example we learn that spiritual power will surely prevail over the forces of evil—but we must take an active part in that struggle."

Today Bonhoeffer continues to inspire Christians around the globe, including those who are persecuted for their faith as well as those who simply want to be more Christlike in their daily lives.

PRESERVING A LIVING HISTORY

In recent years the city of Littleton, Colorado, has been the subject of international media coverage. But most of it hasn't been the kind of coverage that people at the Chamber of Commerce relish.

On April 20, 1999, two troubled teenagers turned Littleton's Columbine High School into a killing ground. After the rampage had ended and the smoke had cleared, twelve students and one teacher were dead, dozens more were wounded, a community was traumatized, and the world wondered why.

A writer for *Time* magazine spoke for many when he said, "With each passing day of shock and grief you could almost hear the church bells tolling in the background, calling the country to a different debate, a careful conversation in which even Presidents and anchormen behave as though they are in the presence of something bigger than they are."

Among the many questions Columbine raised were questions about how two young men from a typical American community could have stored guns, built bombs, and created a Web site and videos full of hate without their parents noticing or taking any action.

The answer was sad but true: many young people live in their own little worlds, and their lives are seldom touched by those who are older and wiser than they are.

That's why a gathering at Littleton's Edwin A. Bemis Public Library on December 1, 2001, was so encouraging.

The library is always a bustling center of community activity, but on that particular day, things were even busier than usual.

Long before the stroke of noon, elderly people in their seventies, eighties, and even nineties parked their cars in the library's lot and made their way inside. Then closer to twelve, local junior- and senior-high-school students began arriving.

To a casual observer, it might have seemed that the library was hosting two events that Saturday: one for seniors and one for students. But in fact, dozens of people of all ages were flocking to a luncheon that celebrated the completion of a yearlong project that brought the two groups together.

The project was the brainchild of two local women who shared an interest in building bridges between the generations and helping community residents explore their shared heritage.

Mary Manley, a graduate student at Denver's Regis University, was working on a thesis and final research project for her master's degree in liberal studies, emphasizing adult learning, training, and development. She titled her thesis: "Oral History: Gateway to Intergenerational Connections."

Phyllis Larison, head of Bemis Library adult services, had already designed the library's World War II Web site on Littleton's Community Network, which was developed in conjunction with Littleton's dedication of a war memorial on Veterans Day 2000.

The women's Regis/Bemis/Vet/Teen Project brought together twelve World War II veterans with nine local students and used the strengths of each group to benefit the community.

The students conducted audiotaped interviews with the veterans, which enabled them to hear vivid stories about a historic event they had previously only read about in school textbooks. The students wrote essays on the veterans' stories as well as on their own reactions to what they gained from the experience.

The library posted the essays on its Web site, along with photos of the veterans and the teens, thus allowing the entire community to join in the experience.

In the long run it was hard to tell whether the teens or the veterans were more excited about the experience. But Aimee Luallin, a Littleton High School freshman, was clearly impressed with the stories she heard from Army Air Corps veteran Paul Hixenbaugh, who received the Silver Star for meritorious rescue efforts in Germany.

"I will never forget what he told me," said Aimee.

A LIVING HISTORY

Writer John Gardner once said this: "History never looks like history when you are living through it. It always looks confusing and messy."

But when history is written down and compressed between the covers of a book, much of the confusion and messiness drains away. As a result, young people who read about World War II in school textbooks rarely grasp the magnitude of these events and the heroism of the people who participated in them.

Making history come alive was one of the major goals of Manley and Larison when they launched the vet/teen oral history project.

"A central goal of the project was to bring youth and seniors together to learn more about the significant offerings each age-group possesses," says Manley.

"The vets were encouraged to share their wisdom and insights from having lived through what has been called the most significant and life-altering twentieth-century event and its aftermath. The teens were prompted to share their perspectives on living in the computer age of the twenty-first century."

Manley also felt an urgent need to preserve veterans' stories at a time when many of these people are dying without leaving a documentary record of their experiences.

"My research indicates that fifteen hundred to eighteen hundred of the five million World War II veterans still alive are dying every day," she says. "Many have never talked to others about the things they experienced."

In addition Manley and Larison wanted to create a bridge between youths and seniors at a time when the two groups have higher suicide rates than other American age-groups.

"I think the teens, especially today in this tumultuous world, are looking for anchors," Manley says. "And the older generation is looking back, trying to make sense of their lives and leave something behind."

One of the people who attended the project's concluding luncheon was Littleton City Manager Jim Woods, who applauded the effort.

"I really see this project as something that will help pass on one generation's experience to another generation," said Woods between bites of salad. "This is a critical thing, this connection between the generations.

"These young people are still at an impressionable age, and if you can help connect them to real people who actually lived through these historic events, you can help the young people have an experience that's more powerful than just reading about something in a textbook.

"In recent years, certain movies have raised the public's awareness, which has helped. But the fact that our country is currently involved in a conflict over terrorism certainly brings things to the front burner. Prior to this, the younger generation hasn't seen much of what war can look like."

A COMMUNITY REMEMBERS

The veterans and teens project isn't the first time Woods and other Littleton residents have sought to celebrate the service of local servicemen and women.

In 1996 the city of Littleton hosted a luncheon for local veterans, and soon after, some of the veterans began wondering if the community should sponsor a memorial of some kind. A committee of half a dozen veterans was established, and Woods began researching the possibility. What he found shocked him.

"When we started out, we had assumed that every town in America must have some kind of World War II memorial," recalled Woods. "Once we began checking things out, we discovered that there were only nine World War II memorials in the country."

Woods and other civic leaders determined that their community, a city of 40,000 in the Denver suburbs, would be the tenth, and the city added public funds to the money that had been raised by the committee, which sold more than 1,400 memorial bricks for $75 each. On Veterans Day in November 2000, the Littleton memorial was unveiled.

"The temperature was near zero, and it was snowing," said Woods. "We didn't think there was going to be anybody there."

Once again, Woods was surprised. More than fifteen hundred people showed up in the Colorado cold to celebrate the unveiling. "The community has completely embraced these men and women," he said. "This effort really struck a chord with people."

The memorial consists of a number of beautiful structures located in a park a short distance from the library. It features plaques containing biographical information on some of the local veterans. Additional information about local veterans can be found on the Littleton Community Network Web site.

INTERVIEWING THE VETERANS

At the December 2001 luncheon, I sat at a table with two of the project participants.

Herb Berner, still lively at age ninety-one, remembers more than his share of hair-raising stories. He was an army sergeant in an intelligence and reconnaissance unit that was responsible for the surrender of twenty thousand German troops.

"I was declared dead four times, and my toes were frostbitten twice," he said. "During the Battle of the Bulge, I was in combat for two hundred and seventy-six successive days. The temperature was eight to ten degrees below zero. The snow was up to our knees. And we didn't have anything to drink because our canteen water was frozen. Things were so cold that one of the men shot a seal, and we used chunks of seal flesh to keep ourselves warmer."

Eric Lomas is thirteen years old. He hasn't had the kinds of life-and-death experiences Berner endured, but now he understands such experiences a lot better.

"I volunteered for this project because it seemed like it would be interesting and it was an opportunity to learn about World War II," said Lomas, a student at St. Mary's Catholic School. "The stories the veterans tell about the war are sad and heartbreaking and funny."

Lomas had read about the war at school, and he had seen the movie *Saving Private Ryan*. But his talks with Berner made the war more personal.

"It's kind of hard to imagine what some of these men have been through," stated Lomas, who is considering a career in the air force. "I learned that there were lots of different battles in countries I didn't know about."

Lomas also made connections between this historic war conducted six decades ago and a more recent conflict.

"I've come to a greater understanding of what war is really like and the harsh reality of what people are going through right now in Afghanistan."

Building Bridges and Understanding

Lomas wasn't the only young person who found the veteran interviews exciting. At the December luncheon, student after student got up to talk about the experience.

Nathan Cyr, a Littleton High School senior, interviewed Bob Bailey, who served in the Army Air Corps. "The most memorable part of the project for me was Bob Bailey himself," said Nathan. "We're friends now, and we've created a little link through this whole experience."

Meaghan Kormondy, an eighth grader at St. Mary's, interviewed Bud Goodwyn, who was a sailor on the USS *England*, a "sub-killer" ship.

"A lot of teenagers don't really understand what these people have gone through in World War II so we can be safe."

Carrie, another St. Mary's eighth grader (who asked that her last name not be used), interviewed Laverne Sarber, who was a member of the WAVES (Women Accepted for Volunteer Emergency Service), a female component of the U.S. Navy.

"It made me realize what it was like to be a woman in this particular war," said Carrie. "My grandmother was in the WAVES, but I never got a chance to talk to her about it."

Holly Verlarde is the editor of the student newspaper at Heritage High School, so conducting interviews is nothing new for her. Still she relished her time with veteran Harry Nuce, who served in the Army Air Corps.

"We bonded immediately, and he told me emotional stories I'll never forget," she said.

What did surprise her was how moved she was by Nuce's stories.

"I think the best thing I gained was that this helped me see beyond my own generation," she said. "Often, we don't appreciate what went before us."

Nuce was grateful for the opportunity to have his memories recorded.

"This is important in my case to help me maybe get the idea to put a bunch of facts down," said the former radar and field artillery officer. "I think of my own father. Dad was in both World War I and World War II, and we don't have a lot of records of what he did."

FAITH AND FREEDOM

In some cases the teens and the veterans were able to talk about some of the deeper spiritual values that are such a powerful influence in life.

Alli Meers, an eighth grader at All Souls Catholic School, interviewed Ralph Mollica, a member of the All Souls parish who survived the attack on Pearl Harbor.

Mollica told Meers about the Mass he wasn't able to attend on the morning of December 7, 1941.

"My barrack bunkmate and I were arguing about which Sunday Mass we should attend—the eight A.M. or the ten A.M.," he said. "The Japanese planes hit at about seven-fifty-five, and we never got there. I still have the bullet that came through my locker."

The eighty-two-year-old grandfather was also able to tell Meers about how his faith has been an anchor in troubled times.

"You realize what your religion means to you after something happens that you can't control," he said. "You understand that the good Lord is still in charge."

For Mary Manley and Phyllis Larison, it was exchanges like this one that made their veteran/teen project so rewarding.

"I do believe that the time and efforts put in by Phyllis and me, as well as by every one of the project participants, will pay off with lasting dividends," says Manley, who graduated from Regis in December 2001 with Jesuit honors, thanks in part to the work she did on the project.

"I think that we have succeeded in providing a model for others to follow for future kindred projects involving not only World War II veterans, but veterans of other wars as well."

To view the project highlighting the Littleton veterans' legacies and insights into the students who interviewed them, visit the Web site www.littleton.org/lcn/governme/wwiimem.html. To view the Littleton World War II Memorial Web Site, from which the project site is an expansion, see www.littleton.org/lcn/governme/wwiimem.htm.

About the Author

Steve Rabey is an award-winning author who has written nearly twenty books for both the ABA and CBA markets as well as more than two thousand articles about religion, spirituality, and popular culture for magazines, Websites, and newspapers. His articles have been published in the *New York Times, Washington Post, Los Angeles Times, Christianity Today, Christian Retailing, Charisma,* and *Publishers Weekly* among many others. Rabey serves as a member of the adjunct faculty at Fuller Theological Seminary.

Hometown: Colorado Springs, Colorado

ACKNOWLEDGMENTS

My heartfelt thanks go to the following people who graciously provided suggestions and information on the men and women whose stories are told in this book (as well as some that aren't):

Marlee Alex, Roger Alliman, Barry Bortnick, Herb Brinks, Danny Byram, Father Timothy Cremeens, Phyllis Douglass, Mike Edwards, Bob Elliott, Larry Eskridge, Arthur Faber, Ross Franklin, Lynn and Gary Ganz, Eric Gorski, Jim Gum, Jay Harmon, Dick Harms, Linda Hoetz Holmes, Jeff Hooten, David Howard, Les Ingram, Douglas L. LeBlanc, Cynthia Martin, Don Martin, Joe McCrane, Jan Moore, Traci Mullins, Tom Neven, David Okamoto, Archie Parrish, Larry Schaad, John Senter, James Skeet, John Michael Talbot, and Marcia Uhlman.

Longtime collaborator Monte Unger helped with editing, and Kristen Lucas at Thomas Nelson made sure text and photos were transformed into a cohesive book.

As always, my loving wife, Lois, was supportive, helpful, and patient.

And veteran editor Victor Oliver of Thomas Nelson, one of the publishing industry's celebrated good guys, came up with the idea for this book and made it happen.

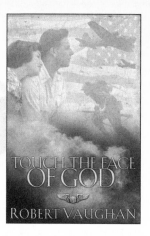

TOUCH THE FACE OF GOD

A WWII NOVEL

In *Touch the Face of God*, Lt. Mark White, a B-17 bomber pilot, meets Emily Hagan only weeks before he ships out to England. They fall in love through letters as each faces the war on separate sides of the Atlantic, but will the war and a misunderstanding tear them apart forever? Lt. Lee Arlington Grant has disappointed his military family by becoming a chaplain instead of a warrior. He hopes his service in the war will heal his rift with his father while he shares Christ with his fellow soldiers—especially Tom Canby. Their lives and the lives of the men and women who fight at their side are interwoven with danger, romance, tragedy, and ultimately hope as the war and their roles in it draw to a close.

Robert Vaughan is a retired military officer with tours in Vietnam, Korea, and Germany, and is the author of more than 250 published works including *The Valkyrie Mandate*, which was nominated for a Pulitzer Prize, and *Andersonville*, which was made into a popular TNT television mini-series. He has written westerns, romances, historicals, and adventures. During his three years in Vietnam he was awarded the Distinguished Flying Cross, the Air Medal with "V" device and 35 oak-leaf clusters, the Purple Heart, the Bronze Star, the Meritorious Service Medal, the Army Commendation Medal, and the Vietnamese Cross of Gallantry.